The World's Stupidest MEN

BARB KARG, RICK SUTHERLAND,
AND DIANA BRISCOE

Published by
Adams Media, an F+W Publications Company
57 Littlefield Street, Avon, MA 02322. U.S.A.
www.adamsmedia.com

Originally published by Michael O'Mara Books Ltd.
9 Lion Yard, Tremadoc Road
London SW4 7NQ
England

ISBN 10: 1-59869-594-0
ISBN 13: 978-1-59869-594-6

Printed in Canada
J I H G F E D C B A

Library of Congress Cataloging-in-Publication Data
is available from the publisher.

This book is aptly and lovingly dedicated to every individual who has ever had to deal with a stupid man. It's also dedicated to the world's greatest scientists in the hope that future generations will benefit from the advancement of gene replacement therapy.

Acknowledgments

Writing and producing a book is never an easy endeavor and *The World's Stupidest Men!* is no exception to the rule. Thankfully, we're surrounded by a host of exceptional individuals who it is our privilege to know and to work with. For starters, we'd like to thank the fine folks at Adams Media with whom we've had the pleasure of working for many years. We offer our highest regards to director of innovation Paula Munier, a brilliant gal whose *joie de vivre* we appreciate and who we adore way more than cabernet and chocolate (and *that's* saying something!). We also salute Brendan O'Neill for his constant dedication, tenacity, and above all his sense of humor on each and every project (and for the record, the contents of this book do *not* apply to him). You guys are the best! As always, we also offer our sincere thanks to editorial director extraordinaire Laura Daly, copy chief Sheila Zwiebel, director of manufacturing Sue Beale, proofer Catherine Forrest Getzie, and senior designer Colleen Cunningham for their tireless and exceptional work. You guys are a fabulous team and we greatly appreciate everything you do.

On the homefront, we forever have the unending support of our families and friends, all of whom we would be lost without and who know that we've never *ever* done anything stupid. (Yeah, right!) Our thanks to Ma, Pop, Dad, Chris, Glen, Anne, Terry, Kathy, the Blonde Bombshell, Ellen and Jim, Jeans and Jim, Karla, Jim V., Linda B., and the Scribe Tribe. You guys have all been a constant support and we consider your love and friendship some of the greatest gifts we could ever hope for. We love you all very much.

We'd like to give a special shout to Chris Grant and Arjean Spaite, and as always to Trudi Karg and Ellen Weider for plowing through our endless humorous rantings and keeping us on the straight and narrow. To Chris, we'd like to offer additional accolades for her exceptional research, made all the better by the fact that being pregnant with twin boys gave her particular motivation for exploring male stupidity. And last, but certainly not least, we thank our flurry of four-legged children, Piper Maru, Jazz, Jinks, Maya, and Scout, who see us through thick and thin, keep us on our toes 24/7, and forever bring joy to our every waking moment. And our dear Sasha, Harley, and Mog who are always in our thoughts.

Many thanks to all of you!
Barb and Rick

Introduction

Man (maan):

An adult male member of the species Homo sapiens.

Stupid Man (stoopid maan):

A descendent of Neanderthals who often behaves in a manner akin to his caveman cousin. One who is capable of such lame-brain actions that he doesn't think twice about lighting a bottle rocket from his buttocks.

When it comes to the subjects of men and stupidity, perhaps no one said it any better than Forrest Gump:

"Stupid is as stupid does."

Over the millennia, men have accomplished amazing feats of intelligence, bravery, science, medicine, technology, and world domination. Unfortunately, those days are gone, and the world of chivalry and class is as elusive as Bigfoot and the Holy Grail. Men of the new millennium have suddenly been awakened by a long-dormant gene—the stupid gene—which has turned a large number of them into stark raving dunderheads. Now, that's not to say that all men constantly act on the urge to light their flatulence, or spend a day at the beach wearing a bikini, or even eat beans for dinner so they can take a "bubble" bath, but most have thought about it—whether they're willing to admit it or not.

It's a Dave Barry world, laced with *America's Most Wanted*, and sprinkled with Gary Larson. It's a world of fast cars, easy chicks, and never-ending draft beer—or so they wish. If moronic men were like diamonds, every women would want one. Unfortunately, most women are stuck with one and they're cubic zirconia. It's a statement of fact, one that is verified by years of study and documentation, that men do the stupidest things on the planet. They start wars, they kill things, they light things on fire, they squish, belch, posture, pontificate, and carry on like gaseous clouds in an atmosphere full of fresh air. But we love men, despite their flawed existences and even in spite of the fact that we know damn well that at any given moment they're liable to become a human whoopee cushion. It is on those days, when we realize just how little it takes to keep them amused, that the true nature of men is revealed. They're a mass conglomeration of silly stunts, inane innuendo, and foolhardy diatribe all of which takes place somewhere between Capitol Hill and Willy Wonka's Chocolate Factory.

In this delightfully amusing little tome, you'll find a wide variety of actions, reactions, quotes, questions, ponderances, quizzes, and downright ludicrous things that men have accomplished—or tried to anyway. Call it a Hall of Shame for *Homo sapiens*, and please know that it ain't pretty. These wicked tidbits include:

Stupid Says . . . • Quotes of the truly stupid

Criminal Minds • Absolutely daft criminals

Shallow Thoughts • Ponderances that drive Mr. Stupid insane

Bumper Snickers • Dimwit car decorations

What's Your Sign? • Birdbrain pickup lines

Politically Incorrect • Terms of impairment

Nitwits in the News • Idiot newsmakers

Medical Morons • Stupid male medical nightmares

Dimwit Die Hards • Ways stupid men die

Excuse Me? • Numbskull excuses

Quid Pro Quo • Insightful Q & A

Comparative Evolution • A comparison of single, married, and stupid guys

The Nuthouse • Insane acts by supreme idiots

Lost in Translation • What Mr. Stupid says, and what it *really* means

Stunt Junkies • Ridiculous pranks of the truly stupid

So join us as we explore the dark side of Neanderthal man gone modern. You'll be amused, astounded, baffled, horrified, and you'll laugh your knickers off. And if you're a guy, you'll be happier than a kitten with a Q-tip. Enjoy . . . and may the farce be with you!

The Ten Commandments of Stupid Men

I. Thou shalt not worship false deities save for NFL commentators, NRA officials, and Pamela Anderson.

II. Thou shalt never do card tricks for the buddies you play poker with.

III. Thou shalt always maintain that reading in the bathroom *is* considered multi-tasking.

IV. Thou shalt not under any circumstances give up your *Playboy* stash, remote controls, or John Deere baseball cap collection.

V. Thou shalt never give up the right to belch, whiz, or pass gas in public places.

VI. Thou shalt never trust anything that bleeds for a week and doesn't die.

VII. Thou shalt never reveal the secret handshake of the Royal Order of Water Buffaloes.

VIII. Thou shalt not covet your girlfriend's younger sister unless she's hotter than your girlfriend.

IX. Thou shalt not kill unless hunting cute furry animals, Bigfoot, ex-wives, or Anne Coulter.

X. Thou shalt always remember that if there's a beer, there's a way.

Belly Up to the Bar . . .

If there's one thing that men enjoy more than fast cars and even faster women, it's beer. It's the one constant in their lives. The one thing they can depend on. It won't criticize or nag. And the carbonation goes up their nose if they guzzle. It's the perfect marriage.

"I feel sorry for people who don't drink. When they wake up in the morning, that's as good as they're going to feel all day."

—Frank Sinatra

"When I read about the evils of drinking, I gave up reading."

—Henny Youngman

"Beer is proof that God loves us and wants us to be happy."

—Benjamin Franklin

"Sometimes when I reflect back on all the beer I drink I feel ashamed. Then I look into the glass and think about the workers in the brewery and all of their hopes and dreams. If I didn't drink this beer, they might be out of work and their dreams would be shattered. Then I say to myself, 'It is better that I drink this beer and let their dreams come true than be selfish and worry about my liver.'"

—Jack Handey

Politically Incorrect

That guy fell out of the stupid tree and hit every branch on the way down.

That guy is proof that evolution can go in reverse.

That boy couldn't pour water out of a boot with instructions on the heel!

Stunt Junkies

In a report by the BBC, fifty-seven-year-old Manjit Singh pulled a seven-and-a-half ton Jetstream passenger jet twelve feet with cables attached to his ears at the East Midlands Airport in Leicestershire, England. Mr. Manjit holds dozens of brain numbing records, such as pulling a double decker bus with his hair, and dead lifting 180 pound weights—also with his ears. Manjit claims his motivation for for these stunts is to encourage children to become physically fit. After the stunt, Manjit said: "I have a bit of pain around the ears, but I'm okay." We think his "pain around the ears" may be the sensation of a mental short circuit.

WHAT DOES IT MEAN
WHEN MR. STUPID
IS IN BED GASPING FOR AIR
AND SCREAMING
YOUR NAME?

YOU DIDN'T HOLD
THE PILLOW DOWN
LONG ENOUGH

Shallow Thoughts

Ponderances that drive Mr. Stupid insane!

Why is abbreviation such a long word?

If you're cross-eyed and have dyslexia, do you have perfect vision?

What the hell is a grindstone, and why would you keep your nose on it?

Criminal Minds

In June 2006, police officers staked out a notorious Greensboro, North Carolina, neighborhood in an unmarked van because of numerous reports of break-ins. During the stakeout, detective Dennis Willoughby sat behind tinted windows and watched as two men pulled up and attempted to break into his van. "They got a pretty good shock," said Willoughby, after arresting both of the masterminds and booking them for attempted breaking and entering.

What's Your Sign?

The truly tragic thing about pickup lines is that the majority of halfwits who use them actually think they work!

Am I cute or do you need another drink?

If you were a new hamburger at McDonald's, you'd be McGorgeous.

I'm looking forward to our one-night stand.

Medical Morons

Many of us would rather get run over by a bus than pay a visit to the dentist, but twenty-six-year-old Walter Hallas of Leeds, England, took the phobia to an extreme when he convinced an equally thickheaded buddy to punch him in the jaw in an effort to reduce the pain of a toothache. The guy smacked him. The attempt at pain relief, however, proved unsuccessful. The punch knocked Hallas to the floor where he struck his head and died from a skull fracture. Sadly, with the current state of American dental insurance, Hallas would likely have suffered the same fate had he sought treatment in the U.S.

HOW CAN YOU TELL IF MR. MORON

IS WELL HUNG?

WHEN YOU CAN JUST
B A R E L Y
SLIP YOUR FINGER
IN BETWEEN HIS
NECK AND THE
N O O S E

Can You See Me Now?

Croatian customs officials arrested a twenty-five-year-old man for attempting to smuggle 175 chameleons into the country on a return flight from Thailand. The lizards, commonly known for their ability to change colors and patterns so that they visually merge with surrounding scenery, were found inside the man's suitcase during routine customs inspections at the airport. Officials indicated that the novice smuggler had falsely assumed that the chameleons would naturally blend in with his clothing and essentially become invisible.

Quid Pro Quo

What you ask him:
Can you please clean the toilet?

His answer:
Sure honey.

What he's really thinking:
Isn't that why you're here?

Excuse Me?

What guy isn't full of excuses, especially when it comes to housework, yard work, or anything ranging from going to the mall to writing Christmas cards? The difference between Mr. Normal and Mr. Moron is that the latter actually believes he can get away with it!

I can't wash the car right now, I'm going to meet Britney Spears at AA.

I'm going to the zoo to feed the animal keepers.

I missed? Guess you didn't remind me to put the toilet seat up.

Bumper Snickers!

DON'T BE SEXIST. BROADS HATE IT.

WIFE AND DOG MISSING.
REWARD FOR DOG.

Lost in Translation

Mr. Stupid:
I'm going fishing.

Translation:
I'm going out on a boat all day to get snockered and tell dirty jokes with the guys.

Comparative Evolution

From amoeba to hairy ape to hunky stud, man has learned to interact with the fairer sex on myriad levels. The single guy has a set of rules that will find him the woman of his dreams. The married man has a method for maintaining his ideal relationship. The stupid guy is just trying to get laid.

Single guy:
I love you.

Married guy:
You know I love you.

Stupid guy:
I love Baywatch.

The Nuthouse

A hot-headed barber armed with a pair of scissors is never a good combination. Believe it or not, an Amsterdam barber was arrested in June 2007 for stabbing a customer in a dispute over a pair of glasses. It was the second time that the shear wielding barber was involved in a violent barbershop altercation. In 2000, he stabbed and killed a client with his scissors, but was acquitted because his lawyers argued he was attacked by his drunken customer and acted in self defense. As for his second bout of shear madness, prosecutors are deciding whether to charge the crazy coifster with attempted manslaughter.

Stupid Says . . .

"I have never been jealous. Not even when my dad finished fifth grade a year before I did."

—Jeff Foxworthy

Yuletide Cheer

It's Christmas Day and a doctor, a lawyer, and a redneck are buying hotdogs from a vendor when a bus suddenly runs them over. Upon their arrival at the Pearly Gates they're greeted by St. Peter, who informs them that if they wish to gain entrance into heaven they must give him an object that represents Christmas.

The doctor reaches into his medical bag and pulls out a small wreath. St. Peter smiles. "Welcome to heaven."

Then the lawyer approaches the gate. He opens his briefcase and pulls out a Santa hat. Again, St. Peter smiles. "Welcome to heaven."

Then it's the redneck's turn. First he looks all around the entrance, but he can't find any type of holiday item. He begins to panic, but suddenly remembers something. He pats down all of his clothing and finally pulls a pair of pantyhose out of his jacket pocket.

St. Peter scowls. "I'm sorry, but how exactly do those represent the Yuletide holiday?"

The redneck grins. "They're Carol's."

WHY DOES MR. MORON
W H I S T L E
WHEN HE'S SITTING ON THE LOO?

SO HE CAN REMEMBER
WHICH END
HE HAS TO WIPE

Top Ten Signs that Mr. Nimrod Is Having a Bad Day:

1. He puts Preparation H on his toothbrush by mistake, and doesn't notice. Then he can't figure out why his arse feels so minty fresh.
2. He arrives at work and finds a *60 Minutes* news team waiting at his office.
3. The Zippy Mart runs out of Budweiser.
4. His blind date turns out to be his ex-wife.
5. He calls his answering service and they tell him it's none of his business.
6. He tells his wife he'd like to eat out, and when he gets home there's a sandwich on the front porch.
7. He calls the "girl" he had a one-night stand with and finds out her name is Bubba.
8. He starts to put on the clothes he wore home from last night's shindig and realizes there aren't any.
9. He calls suicide prevention and they put him on hold.
10. His horn sticks on the freeway behind forty-eight Hell's Angels.

A Royal Puzzle

England's Prince Philip is notorious for verbal gaffes on his travels. Which of the following howlers are actually true?

1. While touring Europe, Prince Philip was quoted saying to another visiting Briton in Hungary: "You can't have been here long—you haven't got a pot belly."
2. Visiting Scotland, Prince Philip allegedly made this comment to a Scottish driving instructor: "How do you keep the natives off the booze long enough to pass the test?"
3. In Canada, Prince Philip bemoaned his royal travel and public affairs duties with this comment: "We don't come here for our health. We can think of other ways of enjoying ourselves."
4. During a visit to the New Welsh Assembly in Cardiff, Wales, Prince Philip reportedly said to a group of deaf children who were standing near a Jamaican steel drum band: "Deaf? No wonder you're deaf standing so close to all that racket."
5. Outside Exeter Cathedral in London, Prince Philip stopped to chat with a blind woman with a seeing eye dog. Philip casually asked her: "Do you know they now have eating dogs for the anorexic?"

Answer: *There's actually only one correct answer—all of them are true. At the current age of eighty-six, Prince Philip often comes across with the haughty patrician acerbity of a cranky old uncle. The British press is constantly on what they refer to as "gaffe alert" in the presence of the Prince, and thankfully, he always manages to come through.*

What's up Your Nose?

Not to be outdone by the show-off who tugged a passenger jet with his ears, a man in China pulled a ton-and-a-half van—with his nose. Fu Yingjie sucked the end of a cord through his nostrils and into his stomach. The free end was then attached to a cable that was in turn connected to the front of a van. Yingjie employed kung fu skills to clamp down on the cord with his stomach muscles and subsequently dragged the van over forty feet. Photographs of the event include Yingjie towing the van and a small group of baffled onlookers who appear to be either transfixed by the spectacle, or preparing to flee with their sanity intact.

Stupid Says . . .

"People shouldn't believe the lies. The reason why I tried to kill that man is because he spat on me. That's the dirtiest thing you can do to a man."

—Bobby Brown

Shallow Thoughts

Ponderances that drive Mr. Stupid insane!

If a parsley farmer gets sued, do his wages get garnished?

If we evolved from monkeys and apes, why are there still monkeys and apes?

Is the hardness of butter directly proportional to the softness of bread?

Lost in Translation

Mr. Stupid:
I need more space.

Translation:
I'm looking for a hotter girlfriend.

Long Arm of the Law

Is there any question that men made up the following laws?

- Georgia law provides that it's a misdemeanor for any citizen to attend church worship on Sunday unless he's equipped with a rifle—and it's loaded.
- In Tennessee, you can't shoot any game other than whales from a moving automobile.
- Kansas law prohibits shooting rabbits from a motorboat.
- In Normal, Illinois, it's against the law to make faces at dogs.
- In Hartford, Connecticut, it's illegal to educate dogs.

Stupid Says . . .

"When you look at Prince Charles, don't you think that someone in the Royal family knew someone in the Royal family?"

—Robin Williams

Quid Pro Quo

What you ask him:
Can we watch Dancing with the Stars?

His answer:
If you'd like to.

What he's really thinking:
I'd rather chew off my left arm than watch Ian Ziering do a rumba.

The Fried Willy Award

After an attempt at duplicating a stupifyingly moronic stunt performed by the geniuses of *Jackass* fame, a Wisconsin man wound up with burned genitals and a trip to the hospital. After watching the stunt in a *Jackass* movie and sucking down a few too many brews, twenty-year-old Jared Anderson volunteered to drop his drawers while forty-three-year-old Randall Peterson hosed down Anderson's privates with a can of lighter fluid and lit them. Peterson was charged with reckless endangerment for his participation. If terminal stupidity was a crime, both of these guys would probably get the chair, but instead, they get the coveted Fried Willy Award!

Dimwit Die Hards

In 1998, six men believed to be illegal aliens from Mexico were hunkering down for a good night's sleep in the great outdoors of Norias, Texas. After giving it some thought, they decided the best place to fall asleep under the stars were the train tracks, likely guided by the false belief that the tracks would protect them from poisonous snakes. Fortunately for them, the vipers didn't get them—but a freight train did when it came barreling down the tracks at 45 m.p.h. A spokesperson for the border patrol said: "The train crew saw some debris on the tracks. That next split-second they saw heads raise up and then six people were killed instantly." As far as we know, no snakes were injured in the tragedy.

Excuse Me?

I'd love to help do the dishes, but I'm late for my colonoscopy.

I'm not feeling well. I think I've got that Ebola virus that's going around.

I can't go to the mall, I've got a terrible case of hanging chads.

Bumper Snickers!

I LOVE CATS. THEY TASTE
JUST LIKE CHICKEN!

I FISH, THEREFORE I LIE.

Stunt Junkies

Inspired by a local television program featuring amazing feats of stupidity, amateur Chinese stuntman Cai Dongsheng trained himself to break nails with his teeth. Dongsheng demonstrated his unique talent in April 2006 by clamping four five-inch long nails into a vise, biting down on them, and breaking all four in half after a little over a minute of resolute jaw grinding. Dongsheng claimed that he had broken over twenty pounds of nails while training in secrecy, because he said somewhat dejectedly: "My family is not supportive."

Nitwits in the News

An Australian sportsman with a bellyful of booze has been credited with catching and landing a four-foot bronze whaler shark—barehanded. Philip Kerkhof was fishing with friends and slugging down vodka on a jetty in South Australia when he spotted the shark—notorious for its dangerously aggressive nature—swimming in the shallows. Acting on impulse, Kerkhof grabbed the bronze whaler by the gills and wrestled it onto shore, suffering only a rip in his pants as the shark attempted to fight back. After the incident, Kerkhof said: "Well, it's amazing what a little vodka does for you." The shark became the featured attraction at a weekend barbecue.

Stupid Says . . .

"We look forward to hearing your vision, so we can more better do our job. That's what I'm telling you."

—George W. Bush

Politically Incorrect

That guy is a few midgets short of a circus.

That boy's elevator doesn't go all the way to the penthouse.

That guy's nuts are so small that squirrels are laughing.

Criminal Minds

In Detroit, two police officers were showing off their patrol car computer equipment to a group of children when R. C. Gaitlin strolled by and stopped to join in. The twenty-one-year-old Gaitlin asked how the computer worked, so the cops asked him for a piece of identification. Gaitlin handed over his driver's license and the officers entered his license information into the system. Moments later, the cops had Gaitlin handcuffed and securely tucked away in the backseat of the patrol car. It appears that the computer worked like a charm, and let the officers know that Mr. Gaitlin was wanted for an armed robbery in St. Louis. What a nimrod!

DID YOU HEAR ABOUT THE **BELIEVE IT OR NOT** SHOW AT THE TRAVELING C I R C U S ?

THEY ACTUALLY HAVE A GUY WHO WAS BORN WITH A WIENER AND A **B R A I N**

Comparative Evolution

Single guy:
Wanna mess around?

Married guy:
Wanna mess around next week?

Stupid guy:
Can you clean up this mess?

Nitwits in the News

It isn't every day that you see a half-naked dude wandering around the office, but it does happen. In 2007, a barely clad goofwad was the cause of a lockdown at a medical building in McMinnville, Oregon. The unidentified lunatic was noticed strolling around on the basement floor of the building wearing nothing but high heels. An astute bystander triggered an alarm which brought responses from the city police and county sheriff's departments. Quick on his feet, the man made his escape before officers arrived, and was last seen making a clattering dash down a hallway in his spiffy heels.

What's Your Sign?

Neanderthal pickup lines.

I have only three months to live, can I spend them with you?

Are you a sergeant? Cause you make my privates stand up straight.

Bond. James Bond.

Bumper Snickers!

EVER STOP TO THINK BUT THEN FORGET TO START AGAIN?

MY OTHER CAR IS A BIG WHEEL.

Politically Incorrect

That guy has an intellect rivaled only by garden tools.

That guy's Slinky is kinked.

The wheel's spinning, but the hamster's dead.

WHY DO BLACK WIDOW SPIDERS
KILL THEIR MALES
AFTER MATING?

TO STOP THE SNORING
BEFORE IT STARTS

Quid Pro Quo

What you ask him:
Can you pick up some tampons for me on your way home?

His answer:
I'd be happy to, dear.

What he's really thinking:
Can't you just stuff a sock in it?

That Figures . . .

Austrian scientists have figured out why so many men are stupid. According to their research, sharing a bed with someone else reduces a man's capacity to perform simple cognitive tests. The study was conducted at the University of Vienna under controlled conditions. Employing the services of a group of subject couples, the pairs were tested after several nights of sleeping together and sleeping separately. The men invariably fared worse after spending the night in the same bed with their partner. The women who participated in the tests were just as bright, whether sleeping apart or not.

Criminal Minds

An Indiana forgery suspect faced seven years in prison in March 2007 for attempting to cash a $50,000 check—from God. Twenty-one-year-old Kevin Russel, was arrested at the Chase Bank in Hobart, Indiana, after police were alerted by a highly skeptical teller. Russel also had several other checks in his possession—ranging in amounts up to $100,000—and all signed: "King Savior, King of Kings, Lord of Lords." Said one of the arresting officers: "I've heard about God offering eternal life, but this is the first time I've heard of him handing out cash."

Lost in Translation

Mr. Stupid:
I'm tall, dark, and handsome.

Translation:
I'm an ex-con and I haven't showered in a week.

What's Your Sign?

Neanderthal pickup lines.

Are you taking applications for a boyfriend?

My bedroom has a very interesting ceiling.

Have you ever played "spank the brunette"?

Easy Come, Easy Go

It's Saturday night and Mr. Stupid is sitting at a bar having a beer and watching a basketball game when a rocket scientist orders a whiskey and sits next to him. After the game is over, the eleven o'clock news begins. The lead story shows a woman standing at the top of the Empire State Building threatening to jump. The scientist turns to Mr. Stupid and bets him twenty bucks that the woman will leap off the building. Mr. Stupid reaches into his wallet and puts twenty bucks on the bar.

"No way she'll jump. That's crazy!" he said confidently.

They watch for several minutes, when finally the distraught woman leaps over the railing and plunges to her death. Mr. Stupid shakes his head and hands his money to the scientist, who immediately starts laughing and hands it back. "I pulled a fast one on you," says the rocketeer. "I saw the news earlier. I knew she was gonna jump."

Mr. Stupid hands his bill back to the scientist. "No. You earned it. I watched the same show, but I just didn't figure that woman was idiotic enough to jump twice."

Shallow Thoughts

Ponderances that drive Mr. Stupid insane!

What is the sound of one hand clapping?

Is there another word for synonym?

Do Roman paramedics refer to IVs as 4s?

Comparative Evolution

Single guy:
Will you marry me?

Married guy:
I'm so glad you married me.

Stupid guy:
How much do you charge?

Stupid Says . . .

"I had rather be an oyster than a man, the most stupid and senseless of animals."

—George Berkeley

Higher Education

Three professors were serving time in a Ugandan prison when the day finally came for them to be executed. First up was a Yale history professor, who was strapped to the chair and asked if he'd like to make a final statement. At once, he began screaming: "I'm a famous historian! You can't execute me! I was framed! Framed!" With that, the executioner flipped the switch, but nothing happened. According to an obscure Ugandan law citing faulty equipment, the professor was set free.

After checking the electric chair, guards brought in a computer science professor from UCLA. After being strapped to the chair he was also asked for his final words. He immediately began yelling: "I taught Bill Gates everything he knows! You can't execute me! I was framed! Framed!" Once again, the executioner flipped the switch, and once again nothing happened. Like his colleague, the professor was immediately released.

Baffled, the guards checked the chair and then brought in an electrical engineering professor from Alabama. He was strapped in, and asked if he had any last words. He looked at an electrical box on the wall.

"I can fix just about anything. If y'all cross that green wire over here with that red one, this chair will work good as new!"

Nitwits in the News

If a man claiming to be a priest accompanied by a woman knocked on a man's door and proceeded to offer that man a naked bath with the woman, wouldn't that be suspicious to most people on the planet? Well apparently not to a lonely sixty-five-year-old retiree living in Linz, Austria, who allowed the couple to run him a bath and was told the woman would be joining him shortly. As the buck nekkid man sat in the tub waiting patiently, the "holy man" and his girlfriend rifled through the man's belongings and stole approximately $200. After ten long minutes, the old man heard the sound of cupboards being opened and closed and finally got suspicious. Emerging from his bath, he chased the couple out of the apartment and phoned the police. The pair was eventually arrested and police said they not only conned four other people, but they also stole from a church collection box. Now if that's not a direct ticket to hell—nothing is.

DID YOU HEAR ABOUT THE **STUPID BUTCHER** WHO BACKED INTO A **MEATGRINDER?**

HE GOT A LITTLE **BEHIND** IN HIS WORK

Excuse Me?

I didn't forget Valentine's Day, I just don't like artificial holidays created by greeting card companies.

I don't have a problem with flatulence, it's just the way I choose to air my grievances.

Sorry I'm late. As it turns out, I'm the weakest link.

What's Your Sign?

Neanderthal pickup lines.

You don't need car keys to drive me crazy.

Can I borrow fifty cents? I want to call my mom and tell her I just met the girl of my dreams.

I may not be Fred Flintstone, but I bet I can make your bed rock.

Top Ten Ways to Drive Mr. Dipstick Bonkers

1. Take away his remote control *and* his Cheetos.
2. Tell him that all the blondes in the world have moved to Siberia.
3. Tell him *Monday Night Football* has been moved to the Lifetime Network.
4. Send him out for a box of tampons.
5. Tell him that condom manufacturers have recalled all of their products because they've mistakenly produced only extra-small rubbers for the last ten years.
6. Remind him that *Family Guy* isn't a real family.
7. Stare at his forehead and ask if his family has a history of baldness.
8. Take him to a Vegan restaurant.
9. Start throwing out his Legos—one piece at a time.
10. Replace all of his Old Milwaukee with Slimfast.

Seeing is Believing

They say love is blind, but in this case love caused a not-so-bright moron to *go* blind. Kwok Waiming, a forty-nine-year-old Hong Kong man, was having an argument with long-time girlfriend Po Shiu-fong when she stabbed him in the left eye with a plastic chopstick. No damage was done because the hot-headed wench had already blinded his left eye six years earlier by poking her finger into it. Common sense would dictate that most men would've left their girlfriend after such life altering incidents, but Waiming decided to hang in there. That is, until another argument over a supposed affair caused Shiu-fong to grab yet another chopstick and poke him in his good right eye. As a result, Waiming lost 10 to 20 percent of his vision in that eye, but at least he finally saw the light and reported the incident to police. He said he never reported the previous assault because it was a "love sacrifice." For her deadly chopstick assault Shiu-fong was given a mere six-month jail sentence. One hopes that Waiming has since found a woman who isn't predisposed to poking his body parts.

Quid Pro Quo

What you ask him:
Could you please take out the trash?

His answer:
Sure honey.

What he's really thinking:
Can't it wait 'til next week?

Stupid Says . . .

"If it doesn't fit, you must acquit."
—Johnnie Cochran

Excuse Me?

I didn't have an affair, that blonde was only in town for an actuary conference.

I didn't mean to insinuate your girlfriend is hot. I simply meant that your girlfriend would be hot if I wasn't with you.

I didn't actually get arrested for soliciting a hooker. It was just a warning.

Criminal Minds

The universal sign for "time out" is usually seen at football and basketball games, but on this odd occasion, police in the Philippines were stunned when a thief they were running after ran out of breath and requested a "time out" by using the famous hand signal. Manila police said the suspect broke into a home and stole two expensive cell phones. When neighbors alerted police, a determined foot pursuit ensued. One arresting officer told a local radio station the perpetrator was "panting and gasping for air when we caught up with him after a 500 meter sprint." No doubt the thief should have considered joining Jenny Craig and taking up Pilates *before* attempting to pull off a robbery.

Politically Incorrect

That dude is one bacon bit shy of a Cobb salad.

The cursor's blinking but the keyboard ain't connected.

That guy's such a genius he thinks Karl Marx is one of the Marx Brothers.

Lost in Translation

Mr. Stupid:
You look really pretty tonight.

Translation:
I'd better get lucky or there won't be a second date.

Dinner at Eight

If you had just killed your wife and stepson and put their bodies in a freezer at your house what would you do? Would you call the police? Run for the border? Or would you proceed to have a dinner party? Well, a Belgian man did just that. After murdering his family he somehow decided it was a good idea to host a dinner party for a few of his nearest and dearest friends. When a thoughtful female guest assisted in the clean-up by washing dishes, she also took leftovers down to the basement to stow in the freezer. Much to her horror, she discovered the two bodies and alerted the other guests who called the authorities. Police believe the wife and boy had been in the freezer for several weeks. Dessert anyone?

WHAT DO YOU DO WHEN

MR. STUPID

THROWS A HAND GRENADE AT YOU?

PULL THE PIN AND THROW IT BACK

Bumper Snickers!

BEAUTY IS IN THE EYE OF THE BEER HOLDER.

I AM WHAT I EAT. CHEAP, FAST, AND EASY.

Shallow Thoughts

Ponderances that drive Mr. Stupid insane!

If turtles don't have shells are they naked or homeless?

How do they get deer to cross the road at deer crossing signs?

Do they call it PMS because Mad Cow Disease was already taken?

Lost in Translation

Mr. Stupid:
Children and small animals love me.

Translation:
I don't do diapers and gerbils make me nervous.

The Daft Side of Sherlock Holmes

Mr. Stupid decided he wanted to become a detective, so he went to his local police station to apply for a job. During his interview with the sergeant, he was required to answer several important questions. "Before we hire you, we need to know that you can think on your feet," said the sergeant.

"No worries," said Mr. Stupid.

The sergeant began his questioning. "What's five plus five?"

"Ten," said Mr. Stupid confidently.

"Next question. What color is grass?"

"Green!" Mr. Stupid blurted excitedly.

"Correct. Who shot Abraham Lincoln?"

Mr. Stupid look baffled. "I don't know."

"Well, when you figure it out, come back and let me know." Mr. Stupid shook the sergeant's hand and gleefully went home to tell his roommate about the interview.

"Did you get the job?" asked the roommate.

"You bet I did." said Mr. Stupid proudly. "They already put me on a case!"

Stunt Junkies

In 2001, a Frenchman with a penchant for performing daredevil stunts was arrested after he botched an attempt to land on the Statute of Liberty with a gas-powered propeller-driven parachute. His plan was to land on Lady Liberty's torch and bungee jump off, but his parachute became entangled and left him dangling about 300 feet above New York Harbor before finally being rescued. Hundreds of tourists were inconvenienced by the statue's evacuation and subsequent three-hour closure.

Forty-one-year-old Thierry Devaux has a history of pulling stupid stunts, including bungee jumps off both the Eiffel Tower and the Golden Gate Bridge. Devaux's lawyer says his client is "An artist whose medium is the bungee cord. He uses this the same way as a painter or a writer or any other artist. He does this because he must do this to express himself." Without a doubt, Michelangelo is turning in his grave as we speak.

Politically Incorrect

That idiot would be out of his depth in a parking lot puddle.

He's one taquito short of a combination plate.

That guy's flashlight is turned on, but the battery's dead.

Dimwit Die Hards

Keith Seymour and friends were enjoying a Fourth of July neighborhood party on Long Island when they decided that fireworks were needed to make the celebration complete. Did they light some small sparklers and stand in awe of their beauty? Nope. Police say Seymour opted to light the fuse of an aerial bomb instead. When the device failed to go off, he stupidly peered inside the mouth of the five-inch mortar tube. Unfortunately, his timing was atrocious, and as he stood over it the charge went kaboom. The blast tore off part of his head and he died instantly. Way to kill a party.

The Nuthouse

Gary Hemsted, a forty-nine-year-old truck driver from Redding, California, was sentenced to ten years in prison for attempted voluntary manslaughter against his wife. What happened was that Hemsted's wife tried to run down the couple's driveway to get away from him after he threatened her, so he got in his pickup truck and went after her. As she attempted to climb over a fence, Hemsted aimed his rifle at her and proclaimed: "You're dead." He then shot her in the thigh. Police pulled up just as the shooting took place. What provoked this violent attack? Was she constantly nagging him? Did he find her in bed with a lover? Did she threaten to take the kids and leave? Nope. He was angry because she failed to renew his driver's license. A trucker by trade, Hemsted was cited for driving with an expired license and he blamed his wife for the lapse. Kinda makes you wonder how he would've reacted if she'd done something *really* bad, like forget to wash his underwear or misplace the remote control.

Quid Pro Quo

What you ask him:
Will you be home by eleven?

His answer:
Of course.

What he's really thinking:
I'll be home when I damn well want to.

Comparative Evolution

Single guy:
Can I take you out to dinner?

Married guy:
What shall I make for dinner?

Stupid guy:
Wanna Happy Meal?

Shallow Thoughts

Ponderances that drive Mr. Stupid insane!

Is antipasto evil?

What was the best thing before sliced bread?

If #2 pencils are the most popular pencils,
why are they still #2?

Bottom's Up!

It's Saturday night and Mr. Moron walks into a bar and orders a shot of tequila. After downing it, he looks into his shirt pocket and quickly asks for another shot. As soon as the bartender pours it, he gulps it down and quickly looks into his shirt pocket. Then he orders another round. After eight more tequila shots, the baffled bartender can no longer keep quiet.

"Pardon me, but why do you keep looking into your shirt pocket?" he inquires.

"I've got a picture of my wife in there," said Mr. Moron. "When she looks good enough, I'll go home."

Excuse Me?

I'm not a couch potato. I'm simply making sure that I test the quality of the cushions before the warranty runs out.

Beer isn't considered alcohol. Technically, it's a carbonated beverage.

I know how to change the toilet paper; I just hate disturbing the bathroom Feng Shui.

WHAT'S THE DIFFERENCE BETWEEN MR. STUPID AND AN OX?

FORTY POUNDS AND A SIX-PACK

What's Your Sign?

Neanderthal pickup lines.

Can I buy you a drink or do you just want the money?

What a coincidence . . . you look exactly like my future wife!

Are you a parking ticket? Because you've got fine written all over you.

Medical Morons

A thirtysomething Floridian yahoo decided in 1994 to get his kicks by sticking little willy into a waist-high suction fitting at a motel swimming pool. Of course the moron got his little thrillseeker stuck. The pool's pump was halted, but that didn't solve the problem so paramedics were called. Unfortunately for the man, wily willy had swelled up and couldn't be extricated. After about a forty-minute struggle the paramedics finally freed willy after a suction fitting was properly lubricated. Mr. Numbnuts was subsequently taken to the hospital where he was treated for his bruised genitalia. No word on the condition of his bruised ego.

Bumper Snickers!

I CONSERVE TOILET PAPER.
I USE BOTH SIDES!

I'M SMILING BECAUSE I'VE GOT NO IDEA WHAT'S GOING ON.

Stupid Says . . .

"Guns have little or nothing to do with juvenile violence. The causes of youth violence are working parents who put their kids into daycare, the teaching of evolution in the schools, and working mothers who take birth control pills."

—Tom Delay on causes of the Columbine High School massacre

Help Wanted!

Twenty-one-year-old Edwin Gaynor had dreams of becoming a police officer so he filled out an application to join the Baltimore Police Department. One of the questions on the application was: Have you ever committed a crime? Gaynor checked "yes," which obviously raised a few eyebrows. During questioning from detectives, Gaynor admitted to a carjacking and robberies in Texas within the same year. A call to Texas authorities and a raid on Gaynor's home, his mother's home, and a storage facility proved that the wannabe cop wasn't lying. Gaynor was arrested and charged with the carjacking (the robberies are still being investigated). A spokesman said: "I guess he got a case of the guilts and wanted to come clean. I've never seen one as easy as this. We have people confess to crimes when they get caught for something. This guy was just applying for a job."

Stunt Junkies

There isn't a woman on the planet who's dumb enough to attempt any of the stupid stunts they see in the movies. A woman may imitate clothes and make-up, but she's not about to light firecrackers from her hiney or decide to go car surfing. Of course, sixteen-year-old Nashville, Tennessee, resident Garrett Shawn Nipper didn't practice that type of obvious discretion. Instead, Nipper decided to go car surfing, which basically involves some idiot standing atop the roof of an automobile as if it were a surfboard. Bad idea. With his friend Joseph Waterman at the wheel of a Saturn sedan and allegedly driving "well over" the 20 m.p.h. speed limit, Nipper began surfing. His big "kahuna-in-crime" apparently didn't notice for a while that Nipper had fallen off the roof and died as a result of slamming into the pavement and a guardrail. Oops. According to Metro police, Nipper was inspired to car surf as a result of the show *Jackass*. Tsk tsk. When will they ever learn?

Politically Incorrect

That moron doesn't have all his dogs on one leash.

He's being repossessed. He forgot to pay his brain bill.

That guy's so daft he thinks virgins come from Virginia.

Nitwits in the News

A budding inventor in the United States has cobbled together a refrigerator that launches beer cans into the hands of thirsty couch potatoes. The mini-fridge, built by John Cromwell, is a remote-controlled, automated device that catapults cans for pre-set distances. Although there is some apparent danger of getting conked on the noggin—especially after a few cold ones—the inventor insists that the danger decreases with practice. Cromwell is test marketing a limited number of beer launchers on his Web site, with an asking price of $1,500. As if women don't have enough to deal with, now they have to worry about flying beer bombs?

Anchor's Away!

Bubba and his pal Mooch went out on their boat to fish and put down a few brews. After several hours of imbibing, the drunken dim-wits failed to notice a storm approaching. The ocean swelled, rain started to pour, and the boat was capsized by an enormous wave.

After floating adrift for several days in a lifeboat, the two men spied a bottle in the water. Mooch picked up the bottle and rubbed it. All of a sudden, a genie appeared.

"Because you released me from my bottle, I will grant you a single wish," said the genie.

Bubba immediately replied. "I wish I had something to drink!"

"So it shall be done," said the genie. He then snapped his fingers and the entire ocean turned from saltwater to beer.

"Dayum," said Mooch as he glared at Bubba. "You got any idea what you just done?"

"Yep," said Bubba. "Now we're gonna have to pee in the boat."

WHY ARE STUPID MEN LIKE
LAWNMOWERS?

THEY'RE HARD TO GET STARTED,
THEY EMIT TOXIC ODORS, AND
HALF THE TIME
THEY DON'T WORK

Criminal Minds

A Des Moines, Iowa, man with a serious nicotine addiction robbed a Citgo Quik Mart of cigarettes, but accidentally dropped his wallet when attempting to make his getaway. As the clerk called police, the moronic robber actually returned to collect his wallet. When he overheard the clerk giving an incorrect description of him to the cops, he generously offered his help.

Clerk to police: "He's about 5'10"."

Robber: "I'm 6'2"."

Clerk: "About 6'2" and about thirty-eight-years-old."

Robber: "I'm thirty-four."

The thief then asked for his wallet back, but a minute later the sheriff arrived and arrested him. It should come as no surprise that despite his unorthodox courtesy he was charged with second-degree robbery.

Comparative Evolution

Single guy:
Do you want to have kids someday?

Married guy:
Let's make a baby.

Stupid guy:
What say I knock you up?

Bumper Snickers!

I GOT A GUN FOR MY WIFE.
BEST TRADE I EVER MADE.

NEVER UNDERESTIMATE THE
POWER OF MY IDIOCY.

Top Ten Stupid Men Christmas Carols

1. Deck the Halls with Bras of Holly
2. Frosty the Hitman
3. Chet's Nuts Roasting on an Open Fire
4. I'm Dreaming of a Smite Christmas
5. It Came Upon a Midnight Beer
6. God Rest Ye Hairy Gentlemen
7. Grandma Got Run over by a Pap Smear
8. Joy to the Hurl
9. Santa Claus is Conning the Town
10. We Three Kings Disoriented Are

What's Your Sign?

Neanderthal pickup lines.

I'm Tom Cruise. Would you like to see my top gun?

I'm a thief. I'm here to steal your heart.

You smell like a sheet of Cling Free on a warm summer day.

The Don't Mess with Texas Lunatics Award

If there's one overwhelming mantra in the Lone Star state it's undoubtedly: "Don't mess with a man's beer." In 2002, forty-two-year-old Steven Brasher was sentenced to life in prison for killing a longtime friend who had the audacity to glug down Brasher's last cold beer. In a taped statement, Brasher said: "There was only two beers left, so I took one and I told Willie not to take my last beer." Willie apparently didn't realize the seriousness of the situation and failed to follow his friend's order. As a result, Brasher shot him in the head, an incident that gives new meaning to the slogan "This Bud's for you."

Quid Pro Quo

What you ask him:
Do these pants make my butt look big?

His answer:
Of course not.

What he's really thinking:
I had a '62 Chevy that was smaller than your caboose.

A Cross to Bear

When most people hold a protest they chant and march with signs. When Gregory Withrow decided to hold a protest outside the California State Capitol he thought the best way to make a statement was to be crucified on a cross. His protest was about U.S. policy in Iraq and immigration, and he also showed his support for white supremacy. To his protest he brought along a partner whose role it was to hammer six-inch nails into Withrow's hands. He apparently planned on being nailed to the cross for six hours. *The Sacramento Bee* reported that Withrow brought notes with him from a Butte County, California, health official saying that Withrow's plan to hurt himself was "thoughtfully considered," and from the Sacramento Parks Department acknowledging that no permit was needed for the crucifixion. Good to know he really thought this thing through, eh?

The Bovine Blues

Farmer John isn't the brightest shovel in the shed, but he's had a really bad morning at his dairy farm. In an attempt to lighten his mood, he's getting drunk at Charlie's Saloon. After serving a few other customers, Charlie walks over to John and brings him a beer.

"It's not even lunch time yet," says Charlie. "What are you doing here?"

John shakes his head and takes a long draft of his beer. "It has been a terrible morning," he says glumly. "I was milking ol' Bessie and right after I filled the bucket she bucked up her left leg and knocked it over."

"So you spilled a little milk," says Charlie. "So what?"

"That ain't the end of it," says John, going on to explain that he took Bessie's left leg and tied it to a post with some rope before milking another bucketful.

"No harm in that," says Charlie.

Farmer John shakes his head. "After I filled that bucket she kicked her right leg and knocked it over just like before. So I tied up her right leg to another post."

Charlie nods. "Sounds reasonable."

"That's what I thought until I filled another bucket and she knocked the damn thing over with her tail."

"So what did you do then?" asks Charlie.

The farmer drank down his beer. "Well, seeing as how I'd used up all my rope, I took off my belt and tied her tail to the rafter."

"That was very MacGyver of you," says Charlie.

"Uh huh. Except my trousers fell down just as my wife walked in the barn."

WHY DOES IT TAKE
MILLIONS OF SPERM FROM
ONE STUPID GUY
TO FERTILIZE ONE EGG?

BECAUSE NONE OF THEM WILL
STOP AND ASK
FOR DIRECTIONS

Excuse Me?

Of course I remember our anniversary. Isn't it this year sometime?

I'm not drunk. I just ate too much of your grandmother's rum cake.

I can't wash the windows right now, I'm studying the chemical interactions of clarified butter.

Stunt Junkies

A Chinese monk has put out a martial arts video showing men how to toughen up their manhood and make them hard as rocks. In the video, Shi Yanwu is seen being kicked in his privates by another man. Other shots include monks dangling in the air by a rope tied to their privates, or pulling a weighty rock with their privates. According to the video, when practicing this form of martial art, "a man can not only protect himself better, but also improve his sexual agility and potency." Yanwu claims he is the last monk who understands this form of art. Perhaps there's a reason for that.

Bumper Snickers!

I LOVE DEFENSELESS ANIMALS—
ESPECIALLY WHEN THEY'RE COVERED
IN BROWN GRAVY!

YOU'RE JUST JEALOUS BECAUSE THE
VOICES ONLY TALK TO ME.

Politically Incorrect

That bloke is several nuts short of a full pouch.

He may be turned on, but his antenna ain't picking up any channels.

That idiot's so dumb he had his Olympic gold medal bronzed.

Dimwit Die Hards

Two Colorado teenagers, seventeen-year-old Samuel Hademark and nineteen-year-old Chris Fuller, had a serious lapse in judgment which cost them their lives. About twenty kids were attending a party in Routt National Forest when the two teens, who were drinking and had marijuana in their systems, climbed atop an oil tank and jumped up and down on it as they were smoking. Unfortunately, the tank exploded and both boys were thrown more than 400 feet to their deaths. Investigators believe that the cigarettes or the ashes possibly caused the vapors to ignite. Once again there is proof positive evidence that smoking kills.

What's Your Sign?

Neanderthal pickup lines.

I suffer from amnesia. Do I come here often?

Do you have a map? I just got lost in your eyes.

The Hershey factory makes millions of kisses a day, but I'm only asking for one.

A Monkey's Uncle

By definition, the word "humble" denotes an individual who shows modesty and does well to downplay their importance in life. Humble would be the last word one would use to describe ultimate über-geek and billionaire Bill Gates. The Microsoft peddler's got no qualms about putting us hard working slogs on the same level as primates. For shame, Mr. Gates. For shame. . . .

"People everywhere love Windows."

"People always fear change. People feared electricity when it was invented, didn't they? People feared coal; they feared gas-powered engines. . . . There will always be ignorance, and ignorance leads to fear. But with time, people will come to accept their silicon masters."

"Microsoft is not about greed. It's about innovation and fairness."

"I have 100 billion dollars. . . . You realize I could spend 3 million dollars a day, every day, for the next 100 years? And that's if I don't make another dime. Tell you what—I'll buy your right arm for a million dollars. I give you a million bucks, and I get to sever your arm right here."

Shallow Thoughts

Ponderances that drive Mr. Stupid insane!

Why aren't hemorrhoids called asteroids?

Why does sour cream have an expiration date?

If a person suffering from multiple personality disorder threatens to commit suicide, is it a hostage situation?

Lost in Translation

Mr. Stupid:
I love to cook.

Translation:
I love the Chinese take-out down the street.

Politically Incorrect

That boy ain't right. The cheese slid off his cracker.

The phone's plugged in, but his receiver is off the hook.

That guy's got too much yardage between his goal posts.

Snow Job

A terrible snowstorm hit just as eight hikers arrived at the top of a mountain. The hikers included one woman and seven stupid men. Knowing they were in trouble, the woman grabbed her satellite phone and called for rescue. Twenty minutes later a helicopter arrived and dropped a rope for them to grab, but due to the severity of the storm all eight of the hikers had to grab the rope and be pulled up simultaneously. So they each grabbed hold of the rope and began their ascent. Halfway up to the helicopter, it became apparent that the rope wasn't going to hold them all, so they decided that one of them was going to have to let go. The stupid men all started whining and bickering among themselves until the woman whistled to get them to shut up. She then made a very impassioned speech, telling the men that she was used to giving up everything for her kids, her husband, and every man she'd ever met. Therefore, she would volunteer to let go of the rope and fall to her death. When she finished her speech, the harebrained half-wits were so impressed they all started clapping their hands.

WHAT'S THE QUICKEST WAY TO MR. STUPID'S H E A R T ?

STRAIGHT THROUGH HIS RIB CAGE

Comparative Evolution

Single guy:
I'd cross oceans for you.

Married guy:
I'd die for you.

Stupid guy:
I'd kill for a night with Paris Hilton.

Stupid Says . . .

"You know, it really doesn't matter what (the media) write as long as you've got a young and beautiful piece of ass."

—Donald Trump

Quid Pro Quo

What you ask him:
Would you like to go to the mall?

His answer:
Do I have to?

What he's really thinking:
If you drag me to the damn shoe store one more time I'll commit hari kari.

Excuse Me?

I didn't forget to bring a condom. I was just being sensitive to your latex allergy.

I swear the chaps in my closet are from my bronco riding days!

I'm not a slob, I just prefer to keep my clothes in plain sight.

Nitwits in the News

Concerned neighbors in a German town called police when they noticed a foul smell permeating their apartment stairwell and also reported that a male tenant had his shades drawn for more than a week and a mailbox brimming with uncollected mail. Police subsequently broke into the apartment fearing they would find a decomposing body. Instead of a corpse, they found a man asleep in his bed with very stinky feet and a pile of filthy, smelly laundry next to him. As it turned out, the lethal gaseous combination was the source of the disgusting odor his neighbors were smelling. Makes you want to take a shower, don't it?

What's Your Sign?

Neanderthal pickup lines.

Your daddy must have been a baker, because you've got an amazing set of buns.

Did it hurt when you fell from heaven?

I lost my puppy, can you help me find her? I think she went into this cheap motel room.

The Name Game

The Smiths were planning an intimate dinner party for their friends and decided to invite Mr. Lamebrain and his wife. During the party, Mr. Smith couldn't help but notice that every time Mr. Lamebrain addressed his wife he used endearing terms like "my love," "sweetheart," and "darling dear." After several hours of hearing this Mr. Smith couldn't help but say something to his friend.

"You know, after all the years you've been married, it's very charming to hear you call your wife all those lovely names," said Mr. Smith.

Mr. Lamebrain shrugged. "I can't help it," he said. "I've forgotten her name."

HOW MANY STUPID MEN DOES IT TAKE TO SCREW IN A

LIGHT BULB?

THREE. ONE TO SCREW IN THE BULB, AND TWO TO LISTEN TO HIM BRAG ABOUT THE SCREWING PART.

Shallow Thoughts

Ponderances that drive Mr. Stupid insane!

When cheese gets its picture taken, what does it say?

Why wouldn't a bear shit in the woods?

If photons have mass, does that mean they're Catholic?

Bumper Snickers!

TODAY'S SUBLIMINAL MESSAGE IS: (*) %
Al Gore

SO YOU'RE A FEMINIST?
ISN'T THAT CUTE!
Rush Limbaugh

Comparative Evolution

Single guy:
Your Chanel No. 5 is driving me wild.

Married guy:
That French perfume smells lovely on you.

Stupid guy:
Is that Pine-Sol you're wearing?

Quid Pro Quo

What you ask him:
How do you like this duck à l'orange?

His answer:
It's great.

What he's really thinking:
Why the hell can't we have tater tots?

Politically Incorrect

That guy's a few peas short of a tuna casserole.

That boy's so dumb that sticks are offended.

That idiot is so ugly that brown paper bags fear him.

The Nuthouse

Many people squeeze a loaf of bread before buying it to see how soft and fresh it is, but Samuel Feldman took his compulsion to the extreme by squeezing and destroying 175 bags of bagels, over 3,000 bags of bread, and 227 bags of dinner rolls in various Philadelphia supermarkets. Packaged cookies with thumbprints through their jelly centers were also attributed to "the squeezer." Feldman was finally nabbed via hidden camera, and was estimated to have caused $8,000 in damage. Charged with criminal mischief, Feldman's lawyer asked the jury to "be tolerant of different styles of bread selection. Not everybody just takes a loaf and puts it in their cart." Feldman was sentenced to six months probation, ordered to pay $1,000 in restitution, and get psychiatric treatment for his compulsion toward mutilating innocent baked goods.

Stunt Junkies

As if the *Guinness Book of World Records* doesn't have enough categories for outright weirdness, a man in the Indian state of Chennai is shooting for a coveted record by threading live snakes through his nostrils and pulling them out of his mouth. The daredevil, who calls himself "Snake Manu," has also swallowed snakes and kept them alive and slithering around inside his stomach for five minutes. (We don't want to know how he gets them out in one piece.) In case you recognize his name—and we hope you don't—Snake Manu made a name for himself in 2003 by sucking down 200 earthworms in thirty seconds. Sadly, none of the worms survived.

Excuse Me?

I wasn't trying to fix the microwave, I merely took it apart to make sure it was safe for you to use.

I'm not spending too much money on beer, I'm just doing my part to save the international economy.

We don't need to go to couples counseling, you just need to find uglier girlfriends.

HOW DO YOU SAVE MR. MORON FROM DROWNING?

TAKE YOUR FOOT OFF HIS HEAD

Criminal Minds

It was after midnight when seventeen-year-old Lakount Maddox biked up to a Taco Bell drive-thru window, waved a very real looking toy gun at an employee, and demanded cash. But Maddox must have forgotten to eat dinner, because rather than take the money and pedal away as fast as he could, the hungry über-daft teen ordered up a chalupa. While he waited for his tasty snack to be made, the staff called police who arrived before the chalupa could be served. Upon spotting the fuzz, Maddox took off on his bike and a hot pursuit ensued with the teen eventually being shot in the arm and leg. Moral of the story: Never rob a fast food joint on an empty stomach.

What's Your Sign?

Neanderthal pickup lines.

Would you mind if I stare at you up close instead of from across the room?

I sure hope you know CPR, because you take my breath away.

I'm sterile.

The Night We Never Met

It was after midnight when two cars had a head-on collision. A woman crawled out of the first car, and a man stumbled out of the other vehicle. Though both of their cars were totaled, the man and the extremely attractive woman managed to escape the accident unscathed. Shaking her head, the woman approached the man. "Can you believe neither of us is injured?" she exclaimed. "Obviously this is a sign from God that you and I are supposed to meet and live happily ever after."

Taken aback, yet completely flattered, the man eagerly replied. "Oh, I totally agree," he blurted out. "This is definitely a sign from God."

The woman smiled and then turned toward her mangled automobile. She then reached down to retrieve a bottle. "Look here—this is further proof. This bottle of Jack Daniels didn't even shatter," she exclaimed. "No doubt God would like for us to drink this and celebrate the fact that we survived."

The man nodded in agreement. She handed him the bottle and he quickly opened it and drank half the contents before giving it back to her. She then promptly put the cap on the bottle and handed it back to him.

The man was confused. "Aren't you going to drink any of it?"

The woman shook her head. "No thanks," she said. "I'm just going to wait for the police."

Comparative Evolution

Single guy:
Want to go to the movies?

Married guy:
Should we rent a movie?

Stupid guy:
Do you mind if I videotape you?

Lost in Translation

Mr. Stupid:
I worship the ground you walk on.

Translation:
I don't care how much you cry, I'm not buying you those Jimmy Choos.

WHY DOES A GUY NAME HIS
MANHOOD?

HE HAS TO BE ON A
FIRST NAME BASIS
WITH THE ONE WHO MAKES ALL HIS
DECISIONS

Shallow Thoughts

Ponderances that drive Mr. Stupid insane!

Why do physicians refer to their businesses as a practice?

To be politically correct, does Santa now have to yell "Ha! Ha! Ha!"?

If it's called tourist season why can't we shoot 'em?

Dimwit Die Hards

In a game of truth or dare always try to pick truth, because a dare could wind up killing you. Michael Gentner, age twenty-three, was hanging out with a few buddies when they dared him to swallow a five-inch fish. Unfortunately, when Genter made the attempt, the fish got caught in his throat and he immediately started gasping for air. His alarmed friends called 911, but upon their arrival paramedics were unable to resuscitate him. Of the truly ironic yet completely true fish tale, a lieutenant in the fire department said: "They could see the tail sticking out of his mouth." Guess that's why they call it see-food!

Top Ten Ways to Make Mr. Daft Cry Like a Baby

1. Inform him your parents are coming to stay with you for six months.
2. Tell him you've set him up on a blind date with Lorena Bobbitt.
3. Let him know that *Monday Night Football* has been canceled and is being replaced by *The Ghost Whisperer.*
4. Hide all the Budweiser and Doritos in the house right before tip-off.
5. Take a welding torch and turn all of his golf clubs into a 3-D rendering of Rosie O'Donnell.
6. Tell him you canceled his *Playboy* subscription and signed him up for *Martha Stewart Living.*
7. For his birthday get him tickets to Celebrities on Ice.
8. Let him know that you sold all his tools and bought stock in the Lifetime Network.
9. Tell him you're leaving him for Pamela Anderson.
10. Tell him that it was announced that beer causes impotency.

Bumper Snickers!

FINANCIAL WHIZ ONBOARD: EXPERT AT WHIZZING AWAY MONEY

MAKE YOURSELF AT HOME! CLEAN MY KITCHEN.

Call Waiting

Sometimes, you've just got to scratch your head and wonder "what the hell was he thinking?" This is one of those times. When investigating an apparent suicide in Newton, North Carolina, police finally came to the conclusion that Ken Barger had been reaching for his telephone to answer a late night call in December of 1992, when he inadvertently grabbed a pistol from the nightstand and shot himself in the head. Do you suppose he was dreaming about shooting Bambi and just got confused? Or did he finally figure out and become suicidal over the terminally mysterious Universal Connectivity charge?

Say Cheese!

Council Grove, Kansas, is a sleepy little town of about 2,300 and just like most small towns, folks who live there know just about everyone else who lives there. This fact alone didn't bode well for Council Grove Sheriff Corky Woodward, who in 1986 rented a video camera and recorder to make a naughty erotic movie of himself and his lovely wife. Unfortunately, the chucklehead forgot to remove the ninety-minute videotape when he returned the equipment. In no time flat, dozens of hot-off-the-press copies circulated throughout the entire community. Under a deluge of steamy gossip, the sheriff and his family pulled up stakes and moved to an unnamed location. If only Paris Hilton would have disappeared as easily.

Politically Incorrect

That dude's been on so many blind dates he should get a free dog.

That guy is hairier than Chewbacca dipped in Rogaine.

He's got an I.Q. of ten, but it takes eleven to grunt.

What's Your Sign?

Neanderthal pickup lines.

I'll tell you the truth. We dated in another life and I dumped you. But that was a terrible mistake and I'm here to make it up to you.

Can I add a branch to your family tree?

You. Me. Handcuffs. Cool Whip. Interested?

Shallow Thoughts

Ponderances that drive Mr. Stupid insane!

If a hog loses its voice does it become disgruntled?

Do cannibals not eat clowns because they taste funny?

What do you do if you witness an endangered animal eating an endangered plant?

NRA Nincompoops

Two stupid hunters decided to go out deer hunting one afternoon. While they were in the middle of the woods, one of them suddenly grabbed his chest and collapsed to the ground. His buddy immediately checked him and found that he was barely breathing. Reaching into his vest he pulled out his satellite phone and called 911.

"Help!" he screamed. "My friend is dead! What can I do?"

"Calm down sir," said the operator. "Take a deep breath and I'll walk you through this trauma."

The hunter took a deep breath. "Okay. I'm ready."

The operator then asked the hunter to calmly explain what happened, which he did. "Alright," she said. "Now the first thing I'd like you to do is to make sure your friend is actually dead."

"Okay," said the hunter. "Gimme a minute." For several seconds the operator heard nothing. Then all of a sudden she heard a single booming gunshot. Seconds later the harebrained hunter got back on the phone.

"Okay," he said confidently. "Now what?"

Medical Moron of the Millennium Award

A sixty-nine-year-old British man decided to take matters into his own hands when he couldn't get relief from his itchy hemorrhoids. When over-the-counter medication wasn't cutting it, he apparently thought it was a good idea to stick a toothbrush up his rectum to get a good scratch. Unfortunately, the rectally challenged bozo ended up going too deep and had to visit his doctor, who was unable to find the foreign object. X-rays at the emergency room showed that the toothbrush was stuck in his pelvis and that surgery was required. The case has been published in the *British Dental Journal* since it is the only documented case where a toothbrush was used in this manner. There's no getting around the joke about not forgetting to brush every night, *butt* this is taking it one step too far.

WHY DID MR. STUPID CROSS THE ROAD?

HE THOUGHT THE CHICKEN WAS A P R O S T I T U T E

Excuse Me?

I swear I didn't know it was cubic zirconia. If I did, I woulda sprung for the $50 ring.

I thought when you wanted me to get Ball Park Franks, you wanted them from Shea Stadium.

I didn't say "those pants make your butt look big." I said, "your butt makes those pants look too small."

Stupid Says . . .

"The only thing that ever consoles man for the stupid things he does is the praise he always gives himself for doing them."

—Oscar Wilde

Politically Incorrect

That idiot's as talented as a one-legged Riverdancer.

There's no doubt that moron is built upside down—his feet smell and his nose runs.

He's a few fries short of a Happy Meal.

Stunt Junkies

Cops and doughnuts are two words that go together like peanut butter and jelly or coffee and cream. Police officers are often chided for their addiction to doughnuts, but this Albuquerque cop needs to enter a twelve-step Doughnuts Anonymous rehab program after the stunt he pulled. The legal lummox was on night patrol in a helicopter when around 1 A.M. his sweet tooth got the better of him and he decided he needed to make a doughnut run. With tax dollars hard at work, he and his pilot circled a Krispy Kreme doughnut shop and landed in a nearby field. After grabbing an even dozen, they took off and resumed their patrol.

A police department spokesman said: "I don't know whose brain child it was, but it's quite an ugly child." A Krispy Kreme employee defended his dedicated customer by saying: "Cops got to eat too." The officer and the pilot faced disciplinary action, their stunt once again giving new meaning to the motto "protect and serve."

The Nuthouse

It isn't uncommon for the legendary doo-doo to hit the fan, but when it hits humans, things inevitably get ugly. James Beal, a sixty-two-year-old ex-Michigan postal worker, was sentenced to eighteen months in prison for throwing buckets of porcupine feces, parasites, and worms at his coworkers after he was fired. Beal's eruption left four people covered from head to toe with the despicable mess, which required a hazmat team to handle the clean-up. The disgruntled Beal was angry over being fired for poor job performance—after less than a week. Thanks to Beal's actions, he has lent more credence to the term "going postal."

Comparative Evolution

Single guy:
I've got two tickets to Cirque du Soleil.

Married guy:
I've got two tickets to the clam bake.

Stupid guy:
I've got forty-eight unpaid parking tickets.

Horsing Around

Mr. Stupid was driving down a country road one sunny afternoon taking photographs of the scenery with his new camera when he spied two horses, one black and one white, in a beautiful green pasture. He pulled to the side of the road and got out of his car. The white horse walked toward him and stood a few feet away on the other side of the fence as the man fumbled repeatedly with his camera, unable to see anything but blackness through the viewfinder.

"You need to take the lens cap off."

Startled, Mr. Stupid looked around but saw no one. Undeterred, he held the camera to his eye but still couldn't see anything. Once again, he heard a voice speak.

"You need to take the lens cap off."

This time he spun around, nervously searching for the source, but again no one was around. As he started to raise the camera again, he could clearly see the horse's mouth move.

"I told you, you need to take the lens cap off."

Shocked, Mr. Stupid looked down at his camera, and sure enough the lens cap was still attached. He removed it and looked through the viewfinder to see the horse giving him a magnificent pose. Mr. Stupid snapped the photograph, and the horse snorted, shook his mane, and trotted off. Baffled by the incident, Mr. Stupid drove to a roadside tavern. He went inside and immediately approached the bartender.

"You're going to think I'm crazy," he said. "But as I was driving into town here, I stopped to take a picture of a couple of horses in a pasture. I was having trouble with my camera, and this horse came over and I swear, it told me what was wrong."

The bartender nonchalantly continued his work. "There were two horses?"

Mr. Stupid nodded.

"A black one and a white one?"

"Yes!" said Mr. Stupid excitedly.

"Which one told you what your problem was?"

"The white one."

"You got lucky," the bartender remarked.

"How so?"

"Well, that black horse doesn't know a damn thing about cameras."

WHY DID GOD GIVE MEN A SLIGHTLY HIGHER I.Q. THAN HORSES?

HE DIDN'T WANT THEM POOPING IN THE STREET DURING PARADES

Quid Pro Quo

What you ask him:
How much do you love me?

His answer:
More than all the stars in the sky.

What he's really thinking:
Not as much as I love my truck.

Nitwits in the News

A Michigan police officer resigned following a 911 call he made after he and his wife got high on pot-laced brownies. Edward Sanchez placed the call in April 2006, telling the emergency dispatcher that he suspected he and his wife were overdosing on marijuana. "I think we're dying," he said. "We made brownies and I think we're dead, I really do." Sanchez later admitted he confiscated the pot from suspects, and that he and his wife went all Martha Stewart and added it to their brownie mix. Shockingly, no criminal charges were filed, but dozens of gross stupidity charges are pending.

What's Your Sign?

Neanderthal pickup lines.

Your eyes are as blue as the ocean. And baby, I'm lost at sea.

My name is John. I'm funny, financially stable, and I've got an interesting DNA structure.

I'd marry your cat just to get in the family.

Criminal Minds

The point to making counterfeit bills is to avoid detection that they are fakes. Obviously this fact was lost on twenty-two-year-old Earl Devine who should have paid a bit more attention to detail when deciding to pass his counterfeit $100 bills around local bars and stores. What was the tip off? A bartender with a keen eye noticed that Abraham Lincoln's face was on the $100 bill instead of Benjamin Franklin. Oops! Devine was arrested and charged with four counts of forgery and four counts of theft. No telling if anyone ever questioned the $1,000 bills he created with Clinton's face on the front.

The One That Got Away . . . With Murder

You'd hope that there would be a limit as to how far a guy would go for his sport, but apparently no one told this chowderhead. A dedicated angler to the bitter end, forty-seven-year-old Franc Filipic hooked a gigantic sheatfish (similar to a catfish) in an eastern Slovenian lake and reeled it toward shore in a hard fought battle. When Filipic stepped into the water to retrieve his prize, he proudly shouted to a friend: "Now I've got him!"

Wrong!

The feisty fish, estimated at nearly six feet in length, dragged the fisherman under the water, where his body was recovered two days later by rescue divers on August 30, 1998. Do you suppose the sheatfish planned to have Filipic stuffed and mounted?

Lost in Translation

Mr. Stupid:
I'm currently between jobs.

Translation:
My unemployment just ran out.

WHAT'S THE DIFFERENCE BETWEEN MR. MORON AND CHILDBIRTH?

ONE CAN BE TERRIBLY PAINFUL AND UNBEARABLE WHILE THE OTHER IS JUST HAVING A BABY

Top Ten Things Stupid Men Do on a Daily Basis

1. Eat pork rinds and drink Old Milwaukee.
2. Light things on fire.
3. Watch *Jackass* marathons.
4. Belch in public.
5. Use Mother Nature as a public restroom.
6. Scratch. Anywhere. Any time.
7. Insist women refer to their winkies as something grandiose like “Trojan Warrior” or “The Incredible Hulk.”
8. Wear two different colored socks.
9. Take dates to dinner at the Burger King drive-thru.
10. Refer to all women as “girls.”

Comparative Evolution

Single guy:
That was the most amazing sex I've ever had.

Married guy:
When we have sex it's still amazing.

Stupid guy:
Are you done yet?

Bumper Snickers!

I'M JUST DRIVING AROUND TILL A STEADY FAST FOOD JOB BECOMES AVAILABLE.

THE FACE IS FAMILIAR, BUT I CAN'T REMEMBER MY NAME.

Excuse Me?

When I said I wanted to be reincarnated as Jessica Simpson's left stiletto I meant it in a philosophical way.

I didn't say, "Will you marry me?" I said, "Will you carry me?"

But I planned this fishing trip weeks before we saw Brokeback Mountain!

Plumbing the Dumbell Depths

An apprentice plumber has been credited with burning a $10 million mansion to the ground after a soldering mishap. The historic English house, built in 1760, was undergoing some major renovations when a peabrained plumber was given the job of repairing water pipes near the roof. The blaze quickly spread throughout the entire structure, requiring the efforts of over sixty firefighters. The inferno resulted in a total loss of the building. Reports indicate that the rookie plumber was absolutely devastated by the event. Actually, our sympathies are with the youngster as well—we're just wondering who the genius is who cut the poor kid loose with a blow torch. After all, this was his *first* day on the job.

Medical Morons

In a seriously creepy effort to achieve self proclaimed "fulfillment," a Milwaukee, Wisconsin, man spent months trying to convince doctors at the Veterans Affairs Medical Center to amputate one of his limbs. In 2005, after the doctors sanely declined, the determined man packed both of his legs in ice for seven hours, causing such severe frostbite that doctors were forced to remove both legs just above the knee. After the procedure he told the startled physicians he was finally happy because there was something about him that was different, and that people would have to make special accommodations for his disability. It didn't last long—doctors have reported that the nutjob is making disturbing comments about thinking his left arm is no longer necessary. All this just to get a handicapped sticker and a better table at Red Lobster? For shame.

WHY DO STUPID MEN HAVE LITTLE HOLES ALL OVER THEIR FACES?

FROM EATING WITH F O R K S

Dimwit Die Hards

Sometimes the ol' Grim Reaper comes knocking and there's just no getting around the fact that your number's up. Such was the case for thirty-nine-year-old Toronto lawyer Garry Hoy, who in 1993 met his fate at the Toronto Dominion Bank Tower. Hoy, a legal eagle described as "one of the best and brightest" lawyers at the Holden Day Wilson firm was giving a demonsztration to law students who were visiting the Toronto skyscraper. As if tempting fate, Hoy's demonstration involved exhibiting the strength of safety windows, which he'd apparently done on previous occasions. This time, however, when Hoy pushed his shoulder into the glass he broke through and fell, plummeting twenty-four stories into the building's courtyard. Dare we say . . . case dismissed?

Quid Pro Quo

What you ask him:
Will you run down to the store for me?

His answer:
Absolutely!

What he's really thinking:
Good timing, I'm out of Budweiser anyway.

Medical Morons

No doubt you've heard of people showing up in an emergency room with weird things stuck to themselves or suffering as a result of something they've eaten. But in 2001, no one at the Via Christi Regional Medical Center-St. Joseph Campus in Wichita, Kansas, was expecting a twenty-something man who showed up with a wire coat hanger stuck in his throat. What was the man's explanation? He claimed he accidentally swallowed a balloon full of cocaine at a party he attended the previous night, a balloon he alleged was slipped into his drink unbeknownst to him. The following day he tried to pull the balloon out of his throat with a hanger, but it got caught and he couldn't remove it. The man had to have surgery to extract the wire. We might've bought the explanation if that kid was MacGyver, but let's face it, that's a hard story to swallow.

Politically Incorrect

That idiot's brain is like a steel trap—it's rusty and illegal in forty-two states.

That guy's a few feathers short of a full duck.

The only culture that moron has is bacteria.

Bumper Snickers!

I THINK, THEREFORE I'M FEMALE.

SAVE THE WHALES AND COLLECT THE WHOLE SET!

The Nuthouse

When robbing a bank, a criminal's typical disguise usually consists of a ski mask or baseball cap, but in a bizarre hold-up at the Citizens Bank in New Hampshire a creative robber duct taped tree branches and leaves to his body in an effort to conceal his identity. Forty-nine-year-old James Coldwell walked into the bank, waited in line with other customers, and then demanded cash from a teller. Unfortunately, it was not Coldwell's lucky day. Not only did the dye pack explode in his heisted bag, but when police released clips of the suspect to the public, he was recognized, identified, and eventually arrested. In describing the arboreal stick-up, the police sergeant said it best: "He really went out on a limb."

What's Your Sign?

Neanderthal pickup lines.

Pardon me, have you seen my missing Nobel Prize around here anywhere?

You're so hot you melt the plastic in my underwear.

I'm a Love Pirate, and I'm here for your booty!

Dumb and Dumberer

Adam was sitting in the Garden of Eden one day when God suddenly appeared before him. In a booming voice, God informed him that he would answer one crucial question for him.

Adam thought for a second. There were so many things he wanted to know, but there was one thing he wanted to know more than anything else.

"Why did you make Eve so gorgeous?" he asked.

"So you would love her," God replied.

"But God . . . why did you make her so stupid?"

God shook his head. "So she would love you."

Quid Pro Quo

What you ask him:
What are you thinking about?

His answer:
Nothing.

What he's really thinking:
Nothing.

Criminal Minds

Most people know that committing crimes is pretty stupid, but criminals don't let that stop them. In fact, some crooks get a lot stupider after the fact. Take Michael DeMoss of Jacksonville, Florida, for instance. After stealing a classic 1979 Chevy El Camino in May 2007, DeMoss rummaged around in the glove compartment and found the name and telephone number of the owner. Suspecting the guy would probably like to get his car back, DeMoss called and offered to sell it back to him for $500. The owner said it sounded like a great idea and arranged for a meeting. Then he called the cops. When DeMoss and the owner got together to make the deal, the peabrained perp was arrested on the spot. *Duh!*

Excuse Me?

Comparing your girlfriends to a witches' coven is actually a compliment. It means they're spiritual!

I can't leave the house, my horoscope says I'm supposed to have an afternoon full of wild nookie.

My unemployment didn't run out, it was obviously stolen by Peruvian environmental terrorists for their "Save the Llama" campaign.

Stupid Says . . .

"You know, one of the hardest parts of my job is to connect Iraq to the war on terror."

—George W. Bush

Lost in Translation

Mr. Stupid:
Of course I love you.

Translation:
But I love my mistress more.

Scourge of the Clergyman

Imagine that you're in a South Dakota hospital, ailing and nervous. A priest suddenly joins you in your room for pleasantries, and a sense of calm washes over you. Of course, that overwhelming peace quickly shatters when you learn your wallet is missing. Much as one would hope that this is a tall tale, it unfortunately isn't. Just ask forty-year-old Mark Gramm, who was in the Sanford USD Medical Center emergency room in July 2007 when he spent several minutes conversing with "chaplain" Leslie Earl Raymond. No one noticed that he wasn't carrying a bible. And by the time Gramm was discharged and noticed his wallet went *adios*, so did the good chaplain—using his victim's credit cards to buy a host of items including a terrier puppy. Surveillance videos captured the faux priest on a spending spree. Bad enough the moron was impersonating a clergy member, but he's definitely going to hell for buying that poor puppy. If the cops don't throw the book at him—PETA will.

HOW CAN YOU TELL
IF MR. IDIOT IS
A R O U S E D ?

HE'S BREATHING

Politically Incorrect

That guy's so stupid he got fired from the M&M factory because he kept throwing out the Ws.

He's so dimwitted he thinks safe sex is a padded headboard.

That moron is so daft that when he got dementia his I.Q. went up.

Nitwits in the News

A man in China claims that a motorbike accident left him with partial amnesia. He remembers everything about his life—except for his wife. The accident initially left Wei Guangyi with total amnesia, but after two days in the hospital his memory returned, with the exception of anything pertaining to his wife of nine years, Yang Jing. Since returning home Guangyi has insisted on treating his wife as if she were a houseguest. He seems to believe that she is actually a former classmate. Fortunately, because he thinks that she's a guest, he doesn't allow her to do any household chores. As a result of this tragic tale, motorbike sales in China are currently at an all-time high.

Comparative Evolution

Single guy:
I love long romantic walks.

Married guy:
I love sitting on our porch swing.

Stupid guy:
Can I call you a cab?

Shallow Thoughts

Ponderances that drive Mr. Stupid insane!

If you're using invisible ink, how can you tell if you run out?

If a synchronized swimmer drowns, do the rest drown with her?

If a man with no arms has a gun is he considered armed and dangerous?

'Till Death Do Us Part

It was a bad day in Pisa, Italy, when a man threatened to kill himself with a handgun in front of his poor wife. Apparently, Romolo Ribolla was incredibly distraught at his inability to find work in 1981, so distraught that he finally decided to end his life. After a conversation with his dedicated wife, she finally convinced him to stop his self-destructive threats, whereupon Ribolla relented and threw his gun to the floor. But that was only the precursor to the really rotten part of Ribolla's day. When he dropped the weapon, the firearm went off and killed his wife. Holy crostini, Batman!

What's Your Sign?

Neanderthal pickup lines.

I'm new in town. Could you give me directions to your house?

Is there an airport nearby or is that just my heart taking off?

Your parents must be aliens, because there's nothing else like you on Earth!

Lost in Translation

Mr. Stupid:
I love to travel.

Translation:
From the couch to the fridge.

Stunt Junkies

Sitting around on the couch sloshing down a few beers one night proved a little too tame for Bradley Johnson and three of his Ellsworth, Wisconsin, buddies, so they decided to hitch the boring old sofa up to the bumper of a pickup truck and drag it through a cow pasture. You're thinking that wasn't stupid? Well think again. Johnson and two of his dimwit co-conspirators were sitting on the sofa at the time. Ellsworth police were still trying to piece together exactly what happened, but the harebrained stunt ride won Johnson an exciting airlift to St. Paul with critical injuries. The two other couch cowboys were treated for minor injuries, and the driver could face charges, although incredible stupidity isn't necessarily a crime. Thankfully, no cows were reported harmed during the May 2007 joy ride.

High-Priced Horror Show

In a show of hideous frivolity, a Russian billionaire gave his wife a trendy $1 million birthday present: Jennifer Lopez. The ridiculously rich banker, Andrei Melnichenko, booked J. Lo for a private forty-minute birthday gig at his estate in England. Forty minutes? It seems the Melnichenko's developed a taste for bringing in major talent for minor gatherings. Christina Aguilera was the "wedding singer" for their 2005 nuptial celebration, clipping the happy couple for about $2 million bucks. Leading the list of celebrities who have rocked the house for Russians of substantial means, George Michael scored a payday of about $3.5 million by performing at a New Year's Eve bash in Moscow for business tycoon Vladimir Potanin. All this, while the majority of the Russian citizenry waits eight hours in line for a loaf of stale bread.

Nitwits in the News

Prom night can be a magical evening for many graduating teens, but when eighteen-year-old Brian Njau realized he didn't have a ride for himself and his date, he panicked. In an absurd scheme, he carjacked a woman's SUV using an unloaded BB gun. Police found the car the next day in a hotel parking lot where Njau and his friends partied after the prom. Police discovered several items in the car that pointed to Njau, including a camera with pictures of him at the prom. Njau, was arrested and charged with robbery and aggravated assault. Bail was set at $100,000, an awfully high price to pay for prom pictures, wouldn't you say?

Stupid Says . . .

"If I do not return to the pulpit this weekend, millions of people will go to hell."

—Jimmy Swaggart

The Theory of Relativity

Mr. Moron went to see a shrink to find out why his wife was mad at him. "I don't get it," he told the shrink. "Last week my wife and I were having a lovely brunch with my mother-in-law."

"There's nothing wrong with that," said the shrink. "In fact, that's more than most husbands would do."

"I know," said Mr. Moron.

"So what's the problem?" the shrink enquired.

"Well, half way through the meal I asked her if she could please pass the butter."

"What's wrong with that?"

"For some reason my words didn't come out that way," replied Mr. Moron.

"What *did* you say?"

Mr. Moron shrugged. "You're a mad cow and you've completely ruined my life."

Quid Pro Quo

What you ask him:
Can you wash the dishes?

His answer:
Uh huh.

What he's really thinking:
My mother never made me wash the dishes.

Bumper Snickers!

NO, I'M NOT GOING TO THE STORE TO GET TAMPONS FOR MY WIFE.

WORK IS FOR IDIOTS WHO CAN'T LEARN HOW TO FISH.

Lost in Translation

Mr. Stupid:
I'm going to check out some shirts I like.

Translation:
I'm going to a wet T-shirt contest.

Criminal Minds

Two burglars had everything they needed to pull off the perfect heist—door keys, pass codes, and combinations for the safes at Mr. Bigg's Family Fun Center in Colorado Springs, Colorado. They also brought along a truckload of stupidity, backed up by a surprising dose of Internet ingenuity. After waltzing into the amusement center after hours using stolen door keys, the dimwitted duo attempted to disable security cameras by spraying the lenses with WD-40—a clear all-purpose lubricant. While they were at it, they also hosed down a fire alarm, apparently thinking it was also a camera. After the lube job, the thieves headed straight for the security room where three safes were kept, punched in the protection codes, and gained entry.

Once inside, the pair of buffoons spent an hour and fifteen minutes trying to figure out how to open the safes, even though it turned out they had the combinations written down! After nearly calling it quits, one of the morons found an office computer where, according to stored Internet logs, he Googled for information on how to crack a safe. Amusingly, the Web search paid off, and the bumbling duo quickly opened all three safes and made off with an estimated $12,000. According to detectives who are investigating the July 2007 heist, it was obvious that the pair had a lot of inside information and are probably former employees. Investigators also mentioned that the WD-40 actually did a nice job cleaning the lenses—the cameras didn't miss a beat capturing the criminally comedic act.

Politically Incorrect

That man is so stupid he thinks an orgasm is the art of paper folding.

He's so vacant that when you look into his eyes all you see is the back of his head.

That boy's so dumb he thinks artificial turf is for robotic cows.

WHY DID MR. MORON BUY AN ELECTRIC LAWNMOWER?

SO HE COULD FIND HIS WAY BACK TO THE HOUSE

Boys and Their Toys

It was February 1990 when would-be holdup man David Zaback walked right past a marked police car in Renton, Washington, and entered a busy firearms shop. He then pulled a pistol and announced a stickup. Holding true to the adage of "shoot first and ask questions later," several patrons immediately produced weapons of their own, including police officer Timothy Lally and one of the store clerks who exchanged a volley of gunfire with Zaback. No one was hurt during the barrage except the steadfastly stupid Zaback who went down for good with several mortal wounds. Not surprisingly, no one was able to count the number of bullets fired during the short gun battle because there were too many of them. Yet again, another good argument for making it illegal for stupid people to own firearms.

Celebudunce Chicanery

Match the lamebrained ignoramus with their unforgivable behavior.

a. Jude Law
b. Mike Tyson
c. Isaiah Washington
d. Michael Richards
e. Hugh Grant
f. Michael Jackson
g. Woody Allen
h. Prince Harry

1. Got busted for soliciting a Sunset Boulevard lady of the evening.
2. Dangled his child over the side of a hotel balcony railing in Berlin.
3. Showed up to a fancy dress party wearing an SS uniform.
4. Got caught by his long-time girlfriend with salacious Polaroids of the girlfriend's daughter.
5. Was involved in an on-set altercation about a homophobic slur he spouted off at a fellow castmate.
6. Had an illicit affair with his children's nanny.
7. Had an "aural" argument with a fellow sportsman.
8. Launched a deplorable three-minute-long racial tirade at hecklers during a stand-up routine.

Answers: *1-e, 2-f, 3-h, 4-g, 5-c, 6-a, 7-b, 8-f*

The Slick Willy Award for Sheer Stupidity

A Romanian man serving a four-year prison sentence for theft collapsed in agony and was rushed to the hospital after injecting his willy six times with petroleum jelly causing his member to grow in length to twenty centimeters and in width to nine centimeters. Apparently, Cosmil Deliu was planning to celebrate his release from prison with a long sex session. He'd been informed that petroleum jelly was good for sex, but didn't realize that it was only to be used externally. Let's say it all together now: VIAGRA.

What's Your Sign?

Neanderthal pickup lines.

That perfume you're wearing is irresistible. Is it called "Catch of the Day?"

If you were a laser you'd be set on "stunning."

Did I mention that I hold the world's record for sucking a golf ball through a garden hose?

The Kitchen Conundrum

Early one morning after a visit to Starbucks, Mr. Stupid excitedly called his mother to tell her that he'd just met the most perfect woman in the world. But within seconds, he became despondent and asked his mother what he should do. Anxious for her son to meet a lovely girl, she suggested he send her a dozen red roses and an invitation to have a home-cooked dinner at his apartment. The next day he excitedly called his mother and informed her that his dream girl was coming for dinner on Saturday night.

The following Sunday morning, Mr. Stupid's mother phoned him to hear all about his date. When he answered the phone, Mr. Stupid was devastated. "The date was a total catastrophe," he whined. "It was horrible."

"Did she stand you up?" his mother inquired.

"No," he sobbed. "She showed up right on time."

"So what was so bad?"

Mr. Stupid could barely speak. "She refused to cook dinner."

WHAT DO YOU CALL A MAN WITH HALF A BRAIN?

G I F T E D

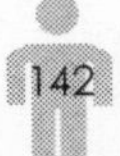

Excuse Me?

I had trouble boiling water for the pasta. I think it's a vast right wing appliance conspiracy.

I'd help with the laundry but my eczema is acting up.

Honestly, when she told me she was a working girl I figured she worked at J.C. Penney.

Politically Incorrect

He's so stupid he actually thinks stores sell cans of whoop ass.

That guy's so dumb he went to the aviary to get a roll of duct tape.

That moron is so dim he thinks WD-40 is a character in Star Wars.

The Nuthouse

Clothing store owner Akira Ishiguro, whose shop is near Tokyo, Japan, became irate when shoppers continually left his store after browsing but failing to make a purchase. Taking matters into his own hands he posted a sign saying "Entry strictly prohibited to shoplifters, browsers, and teasers." When a twenty-six-year-old woman entered the store to look around, she touched a coat but decided not to buy it. Ishiguro immediately flew into a rage and screamed at the woman: "Didn't you see the sign outside? Do you take me for a fool?" He then forced her down on her knees to apologize to him, an act of humiliation in Japan. He also coerced her into putting a $27.12 down payment on the coat. Thankfully, Ishiguro was arrested for allegedly threatening the woman and forcing an apology. The shopping mall association said it had received past complaints on the owner, including an allegation that he locked a woman in the store until she agreed to buy something. Obviously, Ishiguro is unfamiliar with the golden rule of salesmanship—the customer is always right.

Comparative Evolution

Single guy:
You're the smartest woman on the planet.

Married guy:
You're the smartest woman I've ever known.

Stupid guy:
Lucky for you I'm a smartass.

Shallow Thoughts

Ponderances that drive Mr. Stupid insane!

If you choke Papa Smurf, what color does he turn?

When you put in your two cents worth after someone offers: "a penny for your thoughts," what happens to the other penny?

Why are there no Peeping Richards or Peeping Johns?

High Seas Halfwit

A guy walked into a tavern one night and noticed a pirate sitting at the bar. The weathered old scallywag sported an eye-patch, a peg leg, and an enormous rusty hook on his right arm. After buying the old salt a few rounds of grog, he worked up the nerve to ask him about his afflictions.

"So tell me old man. How is it you came to have a peg leg?"

The pirate took a swig of his rum and wiped his mouth. "Aye. T'was a terrible storm we were in one night," he warbled. "A huge wave come about and I was swept overboard. Just as my mates were pulling me onboard, a great white jumped out of the water and bit my leg clean off."

"Wow," said the man. "That's the worst thing I've ever heard. What about your hook?"

The pirate took another swig and lifted his hook in the air. "Aye. T'was an epic battle that was," he said. "Captain ordered us aboard an enemy ship and we battled the scurvy sailors with our broadswords. But just my luck, one of the vermin cut my hand clean off."

His companion gasped. "That's outrageous. It's amazing you survived," the man exclaimed. "How then did you get that eyepatch?"

"Aye," said the dimwitted rogue. "That was a seagull. He pooped in my eye."

The man looked confused. "A seagull pooped in your eye?"

"That it did," said the pirate. "T'was my first day with my new hook."

Quid Pro Quo

What you ask him:
Isn't this diamond ring stunning?

His answer:
Yes, it's lovely.

What he's really thinking:
I think I'll give her my ex-fianceé's engagement ring.

Conjunction Junction

Pretend for a moment that you're standing around waiting for the subway at 51st Street in Manhattan, New York. You think you hear the subway coming, so what do you do? Like most intelligent beings, you take a step back and allow the transport to come to a full stop. Of course, that apparently didn't occur to twenty-year-old Parker T. Hall Houghtaling, who in 2002 was hit by a subway car as he stuck his head out. Miraculously, Houghtaling survived. So what makes the young lad's questionable behavior unique? Three years later, in 2005, the nincompoop once again stuck his head out, this time into the path of an oncoming commuter train in Poughkeepsie. Once again, Houghtaling escaped death, suffering only an injured shoulder, bruises, and fractures to his nose. Houghtaling allegedly didn't remember much about the accident. *Duh!* Perhaps someone should get this guy on the brain donor list before he goes for round three.

Dimwit Die Hards

Diving accidents are unfortunately fairly commonplace, but a Wisconsin man set the bar a little higher by managing to kill himself during a belly-flop contest. The April 2004 event, billed as Diamond Jim Bar's World Belly-Flop Contest was originally supposed to have taken place at the riverfront pier behind the Diamond Jim saloon, but most of the contestants insisted on leaping from a nearby twenty-foot bridge. The first three belly-floppers made the jump with no problem, but according to onlookers, Dorl Gates hit the water with an enormous splash, bobbed up and down a couple of times, and simply disappeared. His body still hasn't been recovered. According to reports, Gates may have spent a bit too much time imbibing in the bar before taking his booze-soaked final flop, and investigators were unclear as to whether or not he could even swim. The unfortunate incident brought the contest to an abrupt halt, but it seems like the decent thing to do would be to give the guy a posthumous belly-flop of death award, don't you think?

Holy Kotex Batman!

The top ten things moronic men are thinking when you ask them to buy feminine protection products.

1. Can't you just stuff a sock in it?
2. Don't you have a girlfriend you can call?
3. I'll drive her to the ER.
4. Don't cotton balls work?
5. Can't you buy them by the case at Costco?
6. If they have wings why can't they fly over here?
7. Don't dinner napkins work in a pinch?
8. Make a list and I'll get my mother to do it.
9. Can't you just turn your underwear inside out?
10. I have no idea what you're talking about. I'm a guy!

Politically Incorrect

That moron is all foam and no beer.

That guy's as smart as bait.

The verdict's in: He's an experiment for a brain-killing virus.

HOW DID THE STUPID GUY PLAN FOR HIS FUTURE?

HE BOUGHT TWO CASES OF BEER INSTEAD OF ONE

Stunt Junkies

Most people settle into a comfortable lawn chair on weekends to have a drink, soak up some rays, and maybe catch a few winks. In July 2007, Bend, Oregon, gas station owner Kent Couch did almost exactly that—except he was wearing a parachute and had 105 helium balloons tied to his chair. Once he was in position, Couch cut the restraining lines and soared over 13,000 feet into the air in an attempt to float clear across the state to Idaho, which would have made his trip the first interstate helium balloon lawn chair expedition in history. The intrepid balloonist had plastic bags holding over twenty gallons of water for ballast and devised a helium release mechanism to adjust his ascents and descents, or ups and downs if you will. After traveling over 190 miles and down to his last few gallons of ballast during the nine-hour flight, Couch was forced to abandon his epic journey just short of his Idaho goal. This was the second flight for Couch, who completed his maiden voyage in 2006, when he was airborne for six hours. As one might expect, the lawn chair lunatic is just itching to plan another attempt.

Nitwits in the News

Alexander Fischer of Berlin, Germany, was so drunk after a booze binge that instead of going home to sleep it off, he went to the train station and mistook the train tracks for his bed. Fischer was fast asleep when a train rolled over him and surprisingly it didn't even wake him up. Fortunately for the twenty-three-year-old moron he was uninjured because he slept between the rails. Workers eventually pulled him from the site. Of his drunken debacle, Fischer said: "I have no memory of lying down on the tracks. I was lucky enough to have not spread any of my limbs over the tracks." Amen to that.

What's Your Sign?

Neanderthal pickup lines.

If I were the king and you were the queen in a cosmic game of chess, would you mate with me?

Is that a Tic Tac in your shirt pocket or are you just glad to see me?

As luck would have it, your hair and my pillow are perfectly color coordinated.

Criminal Minds

We've all had those little Freudian slips every now and again, but here's one that would make even Sigmund spin in his grave. Seeing armed men at a bar in Largo, Florida, desperate patron Dana Shelton telephoned 911. As it turned out, Shelton was surrounded by armed *police officers* who were responding to a reported altercation at the bar. They asked Shelton to move out of the way but he panicked and made the call. The Largo officers scratched their heads and then wrote him a citation for misdemeanor misuse of the 911 service.

Stupid Says . . .

"A study in The Washington Post says that women have better verbal skills than men. I just want to say to the authors of that study: Duh."

—Conan O'Brien

Lost in Translation

Mr. Stupid:
I'm a really romantic guy.

Translation:
I've got twenty bucks in my checking account.

The Blog Victim of the Year Award

James Moss, a Tennessee Highway Patrolman, resigned from his job after allegations that he pulled over porn star Barbie Cummings and was the recipient of oral sex courtesy of the vixen. Cummings claimed she was stopped for doing 92 m.p.h. in a 70 m.p.h. zone. She also claimed that after hearing what business she was in, Moss threw the pain pills he found in her car out into the bushes, and then requested oral compensation. Cummings alleged they performed various naughty acts as Moss shot video and pictures of the liaison. A Highway Patrol spokesman said, "We'll be aggressively pursuing a charge that he destroyed narcotics." Ha! For her part, Cummings stated her submission wasn't to avoid getting the ticket, but rather she wanted something interesting to write about on her blog.

Eggceptional Stupidity

Mr. Dimwit had a terrible problem, so he made an appointment with his doctor. During their meeting he was incredibly distraught.

"What seems to be the problem?" the physician inquired.

"You've got to help me, Doc. I'm having a horrible time with my wife."

The doctor looked puzzled. "Is she ill?"

Mr. Dimwit shook his head. "No. She thinks she's a chicken."

"How long has she had this condition?"

"Ten years," said Mr. Dimwit.

The physician was taken aback. "Why has it taken so long for you to come and see me?"

Mr. Dimwit shrugged. "I needed the eggs."

The Nuthouse

Some guys will do anything to get a woman back and Police Chief John Tuchek of Lanesboro, Minnesota, is no exception. Thinking with his heart and not his brain, he concluded that the best way to get his ex-girlfriend back was to set fire to her apartment building and rush in and rescue her, thereby becoming her ultimate he-man hero. Of course the plan backfired when the blaze got out of hand and demolished several historical buildings. Tuchek, the heartsick arsonist, ended up serving four years in prison. If he's planning another attempt at reconciliation he should perhaps stick with a box of Godiva and a dozen red roses.

Excuse Me?

I thought your new lingerie would fit perfectly. It looked great on the saleswoman.

I never said your mother was a gassy blowbag. I said she had a sassy handbag.

I didn't wreck our car, I was simply renovating it so you'd have something better to drive.

Chain of Fools

They say that art imitates life, and in the case of artist Trevor Corneliusien, that concept proved entirely true. In 2006, Corneliusien decided he was going to do a realistic sketch of his legs chained together, so he went camping in an abandoned mine shaft in Baker, California. To prepare himself to be his own model, Corneliusien chained his legs together at the ankles with a thick chain. Unfortunately, after securing the lock, it dawned on the dimwit that he'd lost the key, thereby assuring that he was now a prisoner of his own art. Stuck in a remote location, Corneliusien had little choice but to put on his shoes and start hopping—yes, hopping—which he did through the boulder- and sand-strewn desert for twelve long hours before reaching a gas station. When paramedics and sheriff's deputies arrived, he was finally released from his bonds courtesy of a pair of bolt cutters. Accompanying the artist on his bunny-hop was his drawing, which according to deputies was a very realistic depiction of someone with their legs in irons. One hopes that Corneliusien's next artistic endeavor has nothing to do with a guillotine.

WHAT HAS EIGHT ARMS

AND AN I.Q. OF EIGHTY-FOUR?

FOUR STUPID MEN

W A T C H I N G

A HOCKEY GAME

Don't Quote Me

Match the peabrained quote to the nutbag who uttered it:

a. Michael Jackson
b. Sammy Davis, Jr.
c. Charles de Gaulle
d. George Carlin
e. Lee Iacocca
f. George Bush
g. Mel Gibson
h. Tommy Lee

1. If God had intended us not to masturbate he would've made our arms shorter.
2. Too many OB/GYN's aren't able to practice their love with women all across the country.
3. We've got to pause and ask ourselves: How much clean air do we need?
4. I've got into midgets recently. They're so fun, those little guys. Every time I see one I just want to pick him up and take him home with me.
5. Feminists don't like me, and I don't like them.
6. Alcohol gives you infinite patience for stupidity.
7. I have a skin disorder that destroys the pigmentation of my skin, it's something that I cannot help.
8. China is a big country, inhabited by many Chinese.

Answers:
1-d, 2-f, 3-e, 4-h, 5-g, 6-b, 7-a, 8-c

Stupid Says . . .

"If you can't beat them, arrange to have them beaten."

—George Carlin

Shallow Thoughts

Ponderances that drive Mr. Stupid insane!

If Polish people are referred to as Poles, why aren't those from Holland referred to as Holes?

Why is it that bankruptcy lawyers actually think they're gonna get paid?

If we aren't supposed to eat animals, why are they made of meat?

Comparative Evolution

Single guy:
Let's go to Cabo for the weekend!

Married guy:
Let's go to Yosemite next summer!

Stupid guy:
Let's go to Arby's tonight!

Off Course

Mr. Lamebrain and his buddy were out golfing on a bright Sunday morning. Mr. Lamebrain had just stepped up to the green to take his shot when he suddenly noticed a hearse, followed by a long funeral procession, driving alongside the golf course. Immediately, he stopped, removed his golf cap, and bowed his head to pray. After the procession passed he resumed his former stance and was about to swing when his buddy spoke up.

"That was amazing," he exclaimed. "That was the most thoughtful thing I've ever witnessed."

Mr. Lamebrain resumed his swing.

"Yeah, I suppose so," he said hitting the ball. "But after all, we were married for thirty-eight years."

What's Your Sign?

Neanderthal pickup lines.

Hey beautiful. My name is Milk. I'll do your body good.

Aren't you dying to know what our children will look like?

You remind me of a championship bass. I don't know whether to mount you or sauté you.

Bumper Snickers!

REAL MEN DON'T ASK FOR DIRECTIONS.

I SUFFER FROM C.R.S.—
CAN'T REMEMBER SQUAT

Rite and Wrong

Freemasons are generally thought to be a charitable bunch of congenial old fellows who throw fish fries, hoot and holler at strippers, and put on funny costumes in secret clubhouses. You don't usually think of them as the type of guys who would pull a gun and blow some poor bloke's head off. But that's more or less what happened at a 2004 initiation ritual in a New York Masonic lodge. Reportedly, part of the secret ritual involved the use of a handgun loaded with blanks, but one of the lodge elders tragically confused the blank pistol with a live semi-automatic weapon. As part of the ceremony, one of the members was banging on a garbage can like a drum while another pointed the gun at the inductee's head. The weapon discharged, killing the new member and bringing the entire proceedings to a shocking halt. Although the incident was deemed accidental, it was no secret that manslaughter charges were filed.

Quid Pro Quo

What you ask him:
What do you think of the Spanish Inquisition?

His answer:
It was a human atrocity.

What he's really thinking:
You're the reincarnation of Torquemada.

Shallow Thoughts

Ponderances that drive Mr. Stupid insane!

Why was Joan of Arc burned at the "steak"?

How do I set a laser printer to stun?

If Helen Keller had ESP, would that mean she had a fourth sense?

Lost in Translation

Mr. Stupid:
That girl at the bar is kinda cute.

Translation:
I'd do her if she wore a bag over her head.

HOW MANY DIMWITTED
B L O K E S
DOES IT TAKE TO REPLACE
A ROLL OF
TOILET PAPER?

UNKNOWN. NO MAN HAS
EVER BEEN SEEN DOING IT

Criminal Minds

Intruders usually break into homes to take things that don't belong to them, but Drake Delande of Willoughby, Ohio, was apparently too tired to pull off a job. After sneaking into a home, Delande was confronted by the owner who asked what he was doing. His reply? "I guess I'm breaking in." The homeowner politely asked him to leave, but found him a short time later napping in one of his bedrooms. After escorting Delande to the door, the owner called police who found the burglar sound asleep on the front porch, thus giving new meaning to the concept of "sleeping on the job."

Shallow Thoughts

Ponderances that drive Mr. Stupid insane!

If the Energizer Bunny beats someone up is he charged with battery?

Do sacred cows make the best hamburgers?

Do you gain weight if you jog backwards?

Stunt Junkies

What would you say about a guy who has the combined strength of Hercules, Superman, and Goliath all centered in one part of his body? Does he have the world's biggest biceps? Is he an Olympic weightlifter? Is he an Iron Man? Nope. He's known as the grandmaster of Iron Crotch—and for good reason. In November 2005, in Fremont, California, Jin-Sheng pulled a rented moving truck several yards over a parking lot with his genitalia. Yes, his genitalia. Not convinced? Iron Crotch is an offshoot of a traditional Chinese practice called Qigong, which is based on a regimen of physical exercise and breath control. Iron Crotch, whose followers train themselves to lift hundreds of pounds using their genitalia (which allegedly increases sexual energy and performance), has a reported international membership of over 60,000. Prior to pulling the truck, Jin-Sheng tied a strip of fabric around the base of his testicles and penis and then had an assistant kick him in the groin. He then strapped his privates to the truck and began pulling. If you're not cringing yet, you will be. The truck actually started rolling forward as the grandmaster leaned against two assistants in order to provide resistance. Ouch! If that isn't enough for you, then suck it up. After his first stunt, he rearranged his lashings so that only his testicles were bound and he pulled the truck again! After his successful tugs of war, Jin-Sheng was reported to have felt no pain and was "warm and comfortable." Originally from Taiwan, Jin-Sheng and his wife, Sandy, who is a *very* happy lady, relocated to San Jose in 2003. All of their four offspring are top notch martial artists. One of Jin-Sheng's greatest students is alleged to have heaved over 660 pounds with *his* junior martial artist. That man was seventy at the time. Jin-Sheng is now fifty-two. Line forms to the left for all those interested in signing up.

Politically Incorrect

That guy's such an idiot he thinks Eskimos get Polaroids if they sit too long.

That halfwit thinks that if you eat pasta and antipasto they cancel each other out.

He thinks foreplay is watching a golf tournament.

Dolls for Dunderheads

Viewers of old *Saturday Night Live* replays are familiar with the amusing image of life-sized blow-up dolls, but Japanese manufacturers have taken the whole concept to a freakish level, transcending the comically cartoonish inflatable variety that look more like wacky pool toys to eerily realistic and anatomically "correct" dolls made with high-tech materials. One Tokyo factory is doing a booming business peddling customized silicon dolls with moving joints and batting eyelashes for prices ranging from $1,000 to nearly $6,000. Some love and silicon-struck studs reportedly have entire harems of the pricey love bundles, bathing, powdering, and perfuming them with a shower of unrequited attention. Creepy yes, but it gets worse. There are companies in Japan who specialize in renting dolls to simpletons who are desperate or just can't make a commitment. The hygienic implications of the business are enough to make one's life-like silicon-based skin crawl. One shop has gone a disturbing step further by renting out private rooms with baths, soft lighting, music, and of course an uncomplaining latex lover. The whole idea is enough to make Barbie blush.

Nitwits in the News

Some men should never be allowed to drink alcohol. Ever. If you need further proof, take note of what ensued in Mülheim, Germany, when a sixty-year-old imbibed to excess. Reports indicate that this moron was apparently too drunk to make it to the loo, so he simply whizzed in his bed. Of course the following morning the dimwit drunkard woke up to soggy bedding. Did he think to drag it all to the laundry room and give it a good wash? Nope. Instead, he put a hair dryer on the bed in a ridiculous attempt to dry things up. Then he left his home. With the dryer running. For an undisclosed amount of time. By the time he got around to returning, his apartment and everything in it were ablaze. Reason #4,864 why stupid men should abstain from alcohol.

Stupid Says . . .

"Until Ace Ventura, no actor had considered talking through his ass."

—Jim Carrey

Face-Off

The year finally arrived when Mr. Stupid turned fifty. Instead of throwing himself a birthday party he decided to have a facelift. After his operation and a month of recuperation he was finally ready to face the public, so he decided to walk down the block to Burger King. While en route, he impulsively flagged down a bicycle courier.

"Pardon me," Mr. Stupid said. "But would you mind telling me how old you think I am?" The courier gave him the once over and then stared at his newly nipped and tucked face. "I'd say you're about thirty-four."

Mr. Stupid started jumping up and down. "Seriously? I just turned fifty!"

Strutting down the street like a puffed peacock, he finally arrived at Burger King. When he got to the front of the line to order his Whopper, he couldn't help but ask the cashier to guess his age. The cashier thought for a second. "Well, I'm guessing you're around twenty-eight." Mr. Stupid screamed. "Twenty-eight! Wow. That's amazing. I just turned fifty!"

After eating his meal he began the walk home. Standing at a bus stop was an old woman and he just couldn't resist asking her to guess his age. "I'm eighty-eight-years-old young man, and my eyesight is extremely poor," she said. "But I can tell your age if you'll allow me to reach into your pants." Taken aback, Mr. Stupid gave it some thought. He looked up and down the street and decided that it would be okay because no one was around. The old woman promptly reached her hand into his pants. "Hmm," she said. "That's interesting." After a moment she removed her hand. "You just turned fifty." Mr. Stupid was stunned. "Wow! How could you possibly know that?" The old woman grinned. "Easy. I was standing behind you at Burger King."

What's Your Sign?

Neanderthal pickup lines.

Are you gonna give me your phone number, or am I gonna have to stalk you?

Could you tell me where they keep the rutabagas?

If you think Chewbacca is hairy, wait till you see my Wookie!

On the Job

The top ten reasons peabrained males have no job security.

1. As employment references they list their mother, their shrink, and O. J. Simpson.
2. They refer to the boss as Mephistopheles.
3. Their parole officer follows them to work to make sure they're not packing heat.
4. In the lunch room they eat fava beans with a nice chianti.
5. When the boss criticizes them, they respond by saying it's a "mute" point.
6. They have obsessive interests in security guards, alarm systems, and methods of egress.
7. Their idea of a coffee break is a Brazilian lap dancer.
8. During company picnics they suggest playing a game called "going postal."
9. They refer to every female in the building as a "honeypot."
10. On their 1040 they claim their multiple personalities as dependents.

Dimwit Die Hards

When it comes to playing hide and seek, some people are really good at the game and others . . . well, not so much. In 2005, police showed up at a home in Debary, Florida, in an effort to collect Earle Herring. The home belonged to his sister, and the cops were there to enforce a court ordered injunction to extricate Herring after a violent domestic dispute. The problem was that Herring was nowhere to be found, so the officers left the scene. When Herring's sister returned to her home over two hours later, she called deputies back to the house believing her brother might have hidden in the attic. Upon their arrival, the officers discovered the attic door securely fastened with electrical wire from the inside, and had to force their way into the room. Once inside, they finally found their anger-prone twit, or rather his body, slowly roasting inside the 100-degree-plus hideout. An autopsy determined that the artful dodger had succumbed to heatstroke. Perhaps next time, the cops should try playing Marco Polo.

Bus-ted!

Every morning when parents put their kids on a school bus, they expect that they'll arrive safely at their school. The last thing they would every think to worry about is a drunk bus driver—or should they? In 2002, Marvin Franks, a Calgary, Alberta, bus driver, risked the lives of forty kids by driving a school bus while under the influence. In the end, it was a frightened but astute thirteen-year-old girl who eventually called 911 after Franks's constant yelling, and when she and her fellow students noticed a funny smell. After authorities contacted the bus company they apprehended Franks, who after blowing into a breathalyzer registered three times the legal limit. He was immediately arrested and charged. To add to his obvious stupidity, the bonehead actually claimed that he reeked of alcohol because he was hung over and that he only drank *two* beers prior to driving his bus route. Yeah, right. In an excuse to end all excuses, Franks claimed the stress of the job caused him to drink, adding: "If you had these kids on your bus, you'd drink too." Oh, and did we mention he'd only been on the job for a month? Moron. . . .

What's Your Sign?

Neanderthal pickup lines.

I've got more money than Trump, would you like to see my tower?

Damn you're sexy. You look just like my mother.

Heaven must be missing an angel. Wanna spread your wings?

Stupid Says . . .

"There's something about me that makes a lot of people want to throw up."

—Pat Boone

Quid Pro Quo

What you ask him:
Do I look like I've lost weight?

His answer:
You do look thinner.

What he's really thinking:
Is that cellulite?

Dimwit Die Hards

It's no mystery that rowdy little kids love to play with fireworks, and occasionally they do manage to do serious damage to themselves when unsupervised, but they've got nothing on two grown men outside of Columbus, Ohio, who killed themselves playing with an invention of their own making. Believe it or not, the dingbat duo of James McKinniss and Jackie Byrd created a homemade two-foot long cannon. In their infinite stupidity, the pair were performing a little show-and-tell with their artillery masterpiece for a large group of bikers during a weekend gathering when suddenly the whole works exploded, sending pieces of metal shrapnel into the vital organs of thirty-nine-year-old McKinniss, and sixty-four-year-old Byrd. Once again, yet another pair of dolts confirm that stupid men are missing the common sense gene. But at least they went out with a bang.

Lost in Translation

Mr. Stupid:
Last night was pure magic!

Translation:
What's your name again?

Ring Around the Rosy

Billy Bob and Little John were sitting in the doctor's office waiting for their appointments when they struck up a conversation. After discussing the weather and the latest local news, Little John asked Billy Bob what it was he was seeing the doctor for. "Well, it's really embarrassing actually," he whispered. "For some reason I've got this red ring around my willy."

"Wow," said Little John. "I can't believe it. I've got a green ring around my willy. What a coincidence!" Both dimwits started laughing, expressing that they felt much better knowing that someone else was suffering from a similar affliction. After a while, a nurse emerged and called Billy Bob in for his appointment. Five minutes later, he walked back into the waiting room with a big smile, and immediately walked over to Little John. "Oh, man. You don't have to worry at all," Billy Bob exclaimed. "The Doc put a little rubbing alcohol on a cloth and the red ring just disappeared. You'll be good as new in no time."

Little John look relieved. "Oh my God. That's the best news I've heard in weeks. Thanks for letting me know." "No problem," said Billy Bob as he waved and departed. A few minutes later, Little John was led into an examination room where the doctor was waiting. After explaining his affliction, he dropped his pants and waited patiently as the doctor examined him. "I'm sorry to have to tell you this, but I'm afraid this is very serious," the physician said solemnly. "We're going to have to amputate."

"Amputate?!" Little John screamed. "What do you mean? Billy Bob told me that all you had to do was wipe it off!"

"I'm very sorry, Little John, but there's a big difference between lipstick and gangrene."

Excuse Me?

I can't mow the lawn, because the garden gnomes are picketing.

My tardiness was inevitable, I was double parked in a parallel universe.

I don't wanna mess around tonight, I'm saving myself for a date with J. Lo.

Lost in Translation

Mr. Stupid:
I really want to get to know the real you.

Translation:
My friends are dying to know if you're a true blonde.

Stupid Says . . .

"If stupidity got us into this mess, then why can't it get us out?"

—Will Rogers

Shallow Thoughts

Ponderances that drive Mr. Stupid insane!

Why do you have to excuse your "French" when you don't speak French?

Where does that leave dad if "mum's" the word?

Why isn't anything "as easy as cake"?

Stunt Junkies

Okay, you're sitting in the bathroom flipping through old copies of *Popular Mechanics* when it suddenly strikes you that bathrooms may be good for something other than the perfect Zen palace for inspirational brainstorming. An Indiana man named Paul Stender found himself overwhelmed by just such an inspiration and set about building his dream. First he purchased a working PortaPotty, then he yanked a Boeing turbo engine out of an old minesweeper, and then he dug up a set of tires. Then, as any true genius would, he set about building what he's dubbed the Port-O-Jet, a 70 m.p.h "loo outta hell." After a few test runs, Stender admitted that his creation has all the road handling characteristics of, well . . . an outhouse. For the record, this wasn't Stender's first mobile experiment. He first became interested in the odd hobby after building a jet-powered school bus. Somehow, a screaming fast portable potty seems to be much more practical. Don't forget to put the lid down!

Stupid Says . . .

"USA Today has come out with a new survey: Apparently three out of four people make up 75 percent of the population."

—David Letterman

What's Your Sign?

Neanderthal pickup lines.

Cupid called. He said to tell you that he needs my heart back.

If you'll be my Dairy Queen, I'll be your Burger King.

The voices in my head told me to come over and talk to you.

Politically Incorrect

He's so stupid he puts ice in his condom to keep the swelling down.

That guy is so dumb that he understands blondes.

That man is such a moron. He actually tried to commit suicide by sticking his head in an Easy Bake Oven.

Medical Morons

By now, just about everyone on the planet has received hundreds of spam e-mails and endured insufferable television commercials promoting the use of "male enhancement products," a term which is, in and of itself, an amusing oxymoron. You're likely also aware that overuse of these products can have some rather painful side effects, something that one particular moron learned the hard way. The *Journal of the American Medical Association* reported a thirty-four-year-old man took matters into his own hands and injected his wee-wee with cocaine in an attempt to increase his sexual performance and enhance the experience. As one might expect, the bonehead entered a New York hospital after suffering an erection that lasted three days. But that wasn't the end of the story. As it turned out major complications set in, and despite doctors' efforts, the sexual Superman's manhood simply fell off. In addition, nine fingers and parts of his legs had to be amputated. At the risk of sounding preachy, let this be a lesson to any idiot trying to find new and interesting ways to narcotically enhance his maleness.

WHY DOES MR. IGNORAMUS KEEP ICE CUBES IN THE FREEZER?

TO KEEP THE REFRIGERATOR COLD

You Only Die Twice

Every so often you have to give points to the Grim Reaper for having a sense of humor. In Iran in 2002, fifty-five-year-old Mohammad Hadi was sentenced to death by hanging for killing a man who was allegedly visiting Hadi so that he could purchase narcotics. Not the brightest murderer on the planet, Hadi initially stashed the corpse in the basement, but when his wife began suffering from nightmares he had to make other arrangements. Thinking his evil deed could avoid being revealed, Hadi lugged the corpse into the desert where it was miraculously tracked down by police. As is customary in Iran, the knuckleheaded killer was ordered to have a public hanging, but just as the noose was tied around his neck, Hadi reportedly suffered a heart attack. Did they go ahead and continue with the execution? Nope. They took him to the hospital for treatment and planned to hang him once he recovered. Final score: Mohammad Hadi: 0. Grim Reaper: 2.

Moronic All-Star Anagrams

1. Dick Cheney
2. Tom Cruise
3. Kevin Federline
4. Robert Blake
5. Bill O'Reilly
6. David Hasselhoff
7. Michael Jackson
8. Phil Spector
9. Tom Sizemore
10. George Michael

a. MEMORIZE SOT
b. ILL BORELILY
c. NASAL CHIMEJOCK
d. CRIPPLE SHOT
e. SCOUR MITE
f. CAGE GRIMEHOLE
g. FADDISH OVAFLESH
h. CHICKEN DYE
i. BLEAT BROKER
j. VERIFIED KENNEL

Answers: 1-i, 2-e, 3-g, 4-h, 5-b, 6-j, 7-f, 8-a, 9-d, 10-c

Shallow Thoughts

Ponderances that drive Mr. Stupid insane!

Where does one purchase a thinking cap?

If you put your best foot forward, how do you choose?

Does "laughing stock" refer to cattle with a sense of humor?

Nitwits in the News

It was after midnight in November of 2005 when twenty-three-year-old Bartosz Drobek, his brother, and another friend decided to see who could spit the farthest. Sitting on the balcony of Drobek's Mt. Prospect, Illinois, apartment, the three men were smoking cigarettes and engaging in a traditionally male saliva hurling contest. Drobek allegedly crouched down low and jumped up in order to gain distance. Unfortunately, he lost his balance and took a dive over the railing, falling two stories until he landed on the pavement. The simpleton spitter was rushed to the hospital, but died the following day. No official word on who won the spitting contest, although with a two-story trajectory it's safe to assume Drobek was in the running.

Comparative Evolution

Single guy:
You're so hot the fire department couldn't cool you down.

Married guy:
You still keep my home fires burning.

Stupid guy:
I'm hot. Grab me a beer, will ya?

The Nuthouse

Earlier in this tome we learned about the mad bread squeezer. Well, we're sorry to report that he's but one of a handful of serial squeezers, and while bread is one thing—breasts are entirely another. Twenty-six-year-old Toronto hospital employee Zachariah Scott took his breast fetish a bit too far when he started posing as a lactation technician at two hospital maternity wards for the sole purpose of copping a few feels. Scott told the new moms that he was there to assist them in breastfeeding their new babies. One hospital realized they had a problem when a mom asked a nurse if she could see Scott again for another consultation and was told that the hospital only has female technicians helping with breastfeeding. The crazed booby hatcher was subsequently caught on hospital security cameras and although he was initially charged with two counts of sexual assault, that number increased as more mamas called police and reported similar accounts after seeing the story on the news. Disgraceful as Scott's behavior was, it could've been much worse. He could've had a prostate fetish.

Sit or Get off the Pot

There are more than a few incidents in life that would cause massive panic in any individual. Things like being trapped on a sinking ship, or falling into a pit of poisonous vipers, or having to live with your mother-in-law for a month. For retired electrical engineer and Colorado resident Bob Dougherty that nightmare became a reality on October 30, 2003, when he innocently used a restroom at a Louisville Home Depot and subsequently realized his buttocks and legs were superglued to the toilet seat. After confirming that he was indeed stuck, Dougherty panicked and thought he was having a heart attack, a very real possibility made worse by the fact that he was still recovering from major heart bypass surgery. For twenty long minutes the poor fella was literally stuck in his stall until a Depot employee entered the loo, but, according to Dougherty, didn't offer to help. Additional employees didn't immediately react to his cries for help, believing the situation to be a hoax.

When Boulder County paramedics eventually arrived, the toilet seat had to be unbolted and both it and Dougherty wheeled out, after which he passed out and the seat was peeled from his hiney. As one might expect, Dougherty sued Home Depot for negligence, citing that he suspected several suspicious juveniles who were in the store possibly pulled the prank. It has been reported that Dougherty is suing for as much as $3 million, and that Home Depot offered a settlement of $2,000. In 2004, Dougherty was accused of pulling a similar stunt in the city of Nederland at their visitor center. Enraged, Dougherty offered to take a polygraph test, which he did in 2005—and passed. Apparently, that's his story and he's sticking to it.

Bumper Snickers!

HE WHO HESITATES IS NOT ONLY LOST,
BUT MILES FROM THE NEXT EXIT.

I'M ALL MALE. BUY ME A BUD
AND I'M YOURS.

Excuse Me?

I don't hate your family. I'm just naturally shy around Plutonians.

Seriously, I would've called you the first time we had hanky panky, but I didn't want to pressure you.

I swear I was only thinking of you. When that girl wanted to introduce me to Victoria's Secret, I didn't realize her name was Victoria.

The "For the Love of God Somebody Please Shut This Guy Up" Award

In a chance encounter with Lord Taylor of Warwick, who is the only black member of Great Britain's House of Lords, Prince Philip innocently asked him: "What exotic part of the world do you come from?" Lord Taylor is reported to have replied simply: "I'm from Birmingham." Apparently Philip is unaware of England's cultural melting pot.

What's Your Sign?

Neanderthal pickup lines.

Would you touch me so I can tell my friends I've been touched by an angel?

Tell me about yourself. Your dreams. Your ambitions. Your phone number.

I'm an organ donor, need anything?

Stupid Says . . .

"Feminism is just a way for ugly women to get into the mainstream of America."

—Rush Limbaugh

Quid Pro Quo

What you ask him:
What's your favorite holiday?

His answer:
Every day with you is a holiday.

What he's really thinking:
It's only 268 days, fourteen hours, and eighteen seconds until Super Bowl Sunday.

Criminal Minds

Two of the unfortunate traits con artists look for in their victims are a highly developed sense of greed coupled with a good dose of gullible stupidity. In 2005, scam artist Franklen Forlemu found the perfect dupe in Nou Chang, the owner of a Coon Rapids, Minnesota, grocery store. It seems that the too clever Mr. Forlemu mentioned to Chang that he'd developed a powerful liquid potion that would turn blank paper into legal cash after hours of soaking. In a demonstration of his daft invention, Forlemu slipped blank pieces of paper between a few real $20 bills, wrapped them in aluminum foil, and donning a breathing mask, carefully poured his concoction over the small stack in a plastic container. After chatting for several hours, the pair unwrapped the package and much to Chang's amazement, all the blanks had magically transformed into hard cash. The excited Mr. Chang raced to the bank and returned to the store with a bigger stack of hundred dollar bills—a total of $70,000.

After going through the tedious process of interleaving blank paper with the small fortune, Forlemu again wrapped the currency in foil and poured in his supernatural brew.

This time, instead of waiting around, sneaky Mr. Forlemu packed up his equipment and said he'd return in a few hours to help unwrap the miraculous windfall. When Forlemu failed to show up, Chang opened the package himself and—you guessed it—found nothing but a stack of soaking wet blank paper. Cheng swallowed his pride and called the cops who quickly arrested Forlemu, who overlooked the cardinal con artist rule of making oneself vanish along with a victim's money. In fact, police captured the fraudster with $76,000 in his possession, suggesting that he'd pulled a previous practice job for the extra six grand. And the concoction Mr. Forlemu had created? After being tested at a forensics laboratory, it turned out to be nothing more than tap water.

Shallow Thoughts

Ponderances that drive Mr. Stupid insane!

If a priest can be defrocked, would a tree surgeon be debarked?

Where do forest rangers go to get away from it all?

Why does "X" mark the spot and not "H" or "Q?"

The Nuthouse

It was only a matter of time before some idiot guy got caught having his way with a mannequin. There's no telling how many times it has happened in history. Unfortunately for a South Dakota teenager, he was the guy who got caught with his pants down. The teen made headlines in November 2005 when he was apprehended by security guards at the Washington Pavilion in Sioux Falls in what can best be described as a compromising position with a poor, defenseless, partially-clad female mannequin. Found on the floor with his pants and undergarments pulled down, the cretinous mannequin stalker was caught and eventually slapped with charges of indecent exposure. (You can say that again.) Police spokespeople politely described the incident as "inappropriate activity between him and the mannequin." The perpetrator, who was eighteen at the time, should be locked up simply because of his name—Michael Plentyhorse. Members of the mannequin union still shudder at the mere mention of his name.

Excuse Me?

It's not that I don't want to vacuum, it's that my religious convictions clearly state "thou shalt not kill," and that includes dust mites.

I don't snore. I'm simply repeating "I love you" in fluent Klingon.

Didn't you clean the toilet last month?

Lost in Translation

Mr. Stupid:
Do you love me more than anything in the world?

Translation:
You need to be out of here before my parole officer stops by.

Comparative Evolution

Single guy:
You look like a supermodel!

Married guy:
You look like Grace Kelly!

Stupid guy:
You look like my mother!

Tech Talk

A billionaire and a computer genius are sitting in a sauna with Mr. Stupid, who's sweating like a stuck hog. All of a sudden the silence is broken by a beeping sound. The billionaire sighs and casually presses a spot on his forearm. Miraculously the beeping stops. "Sorry," he says. "It's my pager. I've got a microchip implanted in my arm." The computer genius nods understandingly while Mr. Stupid stares at the billionaire in disbelief.

A few minutes later, a phone suddenly rings. Without hesitation, the computer genius lifts his arm, puts his palm to his ear, and starts talking. After a minute, he pinches his pinky to end the call. "Sorry," he says. "I hate carrying cell phones so I had a microchip implanted in my hand." The billionaire nods understandingly while Mr. Stupid tries to pick his jaw up off the ground. Feeling just how technologically impaired he is, Mr. Stupid leaves the sauna. A minute later he returns with a long piece of toilet paper sticking from his derriere. Both the billionaire and the computer genius stare in horror at Mr. Stupid.

"Oh, sorry about that," says Mr. Stupid proudly. "I'm getting a fax."

Stunt Junkies

What does it take for guys to fully grasp the concept that stunts are only to be performed by professionals? In an futile attempt to emulate Evel Knievel, a wannabe teenage daredevil rode his bicycle off the top of a twenty-five-foot tall utility shed located on a Pleasanton, California, high school campus. The impressionable young dufus hit the ground front wheel *and* face first, breaking both his wrists and incurring possible spinal cord injuries. His wish to fly was granted as he was airlifted to a nearby hospital. Pleasanton police sergeant Craig Eicher later made the understated observation that "people do some pretty stupid things."

Politically Incorrect

That guy's so dense he joined a French Club to learn how to kiss.

That bonehead is so dumb he thinks hunting trips mean killing cases of Budweiser.

He's so stupid he thinks passing gas means driving past Chevron.

Medical Morons

Eww! Here's a story that mommies won't want the kids to see. According to 2004 news reports, an Austrian physician named Dr. Friedrich Bischinger made the icky claim that picking one's nose and ingesting the results is a great way to strengthen the body's immune system. According to the good doctor, the nostrils act as a filter that collects a variety of helpful bacteria. Not only that, but the claim pointed out that fingers are far more effective than tissue for clearing out nasal debris. The Austrian doc may have been following up on a 1995 study conducted by the University of Wisconsin that focused on the habit of nose-picking, technically known as *rhinotillexomania*, which is more than any of us really needs to know in our lifetime. According to the report, 91 percent of the population admits to picking their noses, with nearly a quarter having at it on a daily basis. Only 8 percent admitted to consuming their discoveries, which must have been disheartening for dear Doctor Bischinger. Of historical interest to nose-picking enthusiasts, papyrus records show that Egyptian pharaoh, Tutankhamen hired a personal nose-picker as part of his staff, and professional pickers were prized by nobility. Apparently, the royal habit fell into disfavor during the days of the Roman Empire in A.D. 300 when Emperor Constantine ordered that anyone caught with a finger buried past the first knuckle was to be executed on the spot. Although nose-picking is commonplace and usually practiced discreetly, it's also disgustingly commonplace to find stupid guys diligently excavating with blissful abandon. Again, more than we needed to know.

Shallow Thoughts

Ponderances that drive Mr. Stupid insane!

If you dream in color is it a pigment of your imagination?

Why do they use sterilized needles to administer lethal injections?

How come no one ever lets the dog out of the bag?

The Wizard of Odd

When it comes right down to it, what teenaged boy doesn't want to drive his father's car? In most circles, it's almost a rite of passage. Of course, being given the honor of driving daddy's vehicle comes with certain responsibilities like keeping it tidy, not speeding, and not killing anyone. When an eighteen-year-old Lithuanian kid hit a pedestrian while driving his father's Audi, he panicked and immediately left the scene of the crime. Was the panic caused by the fact that he hit someone? Nope. Apparently he didn't have a driver's license. When the dimwit driver got home, however, he was stunned to find that the dead victim was still under daddy's Audi—the poor man's feet sticking out from under the car like the Wicked Witch of the East. Once the crime was reported and discovered, police identified the victim as a sixty-four-year-old man whom they believe was lying drunk in the street when he was hit by the car. So exactly why did the teenage twit not have a driver's license? According to Stasys Meliunas, the Rokiskis police chief, the accident was a travesty that clearly exhibited why the dope failed to pass his driver's license test not once or twice—but four times.

Quid Pro Quo

What you ask him:
Are you planning anything for my birthday?

His answer:
Of course. But it's a surprise.

What he's really thinking:
When the hell is your birthday?

What's Your Sign?

Neanderthal pickup lines.

For the love of God, I'm choking! I need mouth-to-mouth quick!

Are you free tonight or will it cost me?

I've got a present for you. You're going to bear my children for the next five years.

Nitwits in the News

Some people are so bloody daft that you just want to shake them silly. In 2002, a Canadian man was pulled over by police near Mississauga. He wasn't speeding. He wasn't driving with his headlights off. But he *was* driving while his nine-year-old son was jumping around on the backseat of the car. After police officers saw the boy unrestrained they pulled the car over. When they approached the vehicle, they were appalled at what they saw. Neither the father nor the son were wearing seatbelts, but a crate of beer was safely buckled up in the passenger seat. Traffic sergeant Cam Woolley told *The Mississauga News*: "It was like this guy cared more for his precious beer bottles getting smashed than he did for his son going through the windshield."

If you happen to meet this moron—shake him silly.

Over My Dead Body

The top ten things Mr. Birdbrain would rather die than do.

1. Watch a synchronized swimming match.
2. Sit through a Lifetime Movie network marathon of Danielle Steel films.
3. Give up his beer can collection.
4. Admit WWE wrestling is staged.
5. Surrender his Super Bowl tickets to attend his grandma's 102nd birthday party.
6. Go to bed sober on New Year's Eve.
7. Allow any female of any species to lay a hand on his remote controls.
8. Listen to the soundtrack to *The Bridges of Madison County.*
9. Separate his whites from his colors when doing laundry.
10. Admit that little willy is in a coma.

Stupid Says . . .

"If there are no stupid questions, then what kind of questions do stupid people ask?"

—Scott Adams

WHAT'S THE DIFFERENCE BETWEEN MR. MORON AND BIGFOOT?

ONE IS COVERED WITH MATTED HAIR AND SMELLS TERRIBLE, THE OTHER HAS BIG FEET

Criminal Minds

It's surprising how many crooks are under the bizarre impression that women think outlaws are hot. After two gunmen held up a U-Haul rental store in Milwaukee, Wisconsin, in May 2007, one of the robbers left immediately. The other one, however, hung around and attempted to make small talk with the woman he'd just robbed, even asking for her phone number! After striking out with the irritated employee, the harebrained thief fled mere moments before the police arrived. So is becoming an armed robber easier than going to *Match.com?*

Comparative Evolution

Single guy:
Would you prefer Dom Perignon with your lobster?

Married guy:
Can I pour you a cabernet with your T-bone?

Stupid guy:
Want a Diet Coke with your Whopper?

Read It and Weep

It must be said that not all who pull bonehead moves are educationally deficient. Case in point—frat boys. College graduates are generally expected to fare economically better in life than their non–higher educated counterparts, but a study conducted by the U.S. Department of Education shows a disturbing trend in just how many skills graduates are seriously lacking. College grads apparently aren't struggling with quantum mechanics or molecular engineering, they're dropping the ball on the most basic skill of all—literacy. The term "proficiently literate" pretty well sums up that ridiculously basic skill set, and a pathetically tiny one-quarter of college grads meet the criteria for literate proficiency. What's worse, the level of expertise shown by current college grads is measurably dropping from the basic know-how graduates possessed just a decade ago. So, if you've handed this book to a recently graduated collegian and find that you're having to explain the elementary concept of "stupid men," don't be overly surprised. In fact, it's probably better that they don't realize the book is about them!

Dimwit Die Hards

People die every day as a result of freak accidents, and for the most part the reason those accidents occur can be surmised. But every so often, you have to scratch your head and wonder what the hell someone was thinking. Case in point, a Louisiana man who was trying to break into his girlfriend's parked car. You might assume he was using the ol' coat hanger trick, but no, this moron used a screwdriver to open the trunk, crawled inside, and was subsequently trapped when the trunk slammed shut. With no emergency latch on the inside, he was trapped for several hours in sweltering heat and perished before anyone realized he was inside. After investigating the incident, the police ruled the death an accident. Lummoxus, the God of Ignoramuses, ruled it an act of supreme stupidity.

Excuse Me?

I need to take a nap, I've got brain gout.

I'm afraid I can't take out the trash today because Mercury is in retrograde.

I need to go out tonight, the boys are having a quiche-making lesson.

Bumper Snickers!

AM I AMBIVALENT? WELL, YES AND NO.

I USED TO BE A LIFEGUARD,
BUT SOME BLUE KID GOT ME FIRED.

The Nuthouse

When you gotta go, you gotta go now! A Fredericksburg, Virginia, woman who stepped out of her house to run a few errands returned to her home to find an intruder making himself at home—on her toilet. After asking the man how long he was going to be, the woman called police. The squatter quickly finished his business and made a hasty retreat before officers arrived. No one was injured in the bizarre occurrence, which was a relief for the homeowner, the cops, and no doubt, the intruder.

Shallow Thoughts

Ponderances that drive Mr. Stupid insane!

Do you have to pay the piper if he's a lousy musician?

If it's raining cats and dogs do you call Animal Control?

If you live from hand to mouth, are you an overeater?

Lost in Translation

Mr. Stupid:
You're the smartest woman I've ever met.

Translation:
I need to find a dumber broad.

Stupid Says . . .

"An empty head is not really empty; it is stuffed with rubbish. Hence the difficulty of forcing anything into it."

—Eric Hoffer

Stunt Junkies

The relative ease of videotaping and posting ridiculously absurd stunts on the Internet has opened a floodgate for youngsters hell-bent on plumbing the depths of outrageous behavior. One of the most recent examples of stupidity floating about in cyberspace is a short film from 2006 documenting some teens' attempt to fire a bottle rocket from a bodily orifice clearly not intended for the purpose. In the nighttime video, a volunteer dropped his trousers and laid in a driveway with his legs thrown above his head while a cohort offered clinical advice on inserting the wooden spine of the rocket into his bum. Then another idiot lit the fuse. Nervous giggles turned to shrieks of pain when the rocket ignited but failed to leave the launch pad, spraying the kid's tender parts with a flaming shower of sparks. The flailing imbecile managed to extricate the incendiary device just moments before it exploded. It could easily be argued that given the metaphorical position of the kid's head at the time, this dimwitted clown not only got a bum deal, but narrowly escaped blowing his brains out. Although by all appearances, he may not have much brain to explode.

Quid Pro Quo

What you ask him:
Do you want to watch a movie tonight on the Lifetime Network?

His answer:
I can't wait.

What he's really thinking:
I'd rather be hanged, drowned, shot, stabbed, drawn and quartered, and burned at the stake all at the same time.

What's Your Sign?

Neanderthal pickup lines.

Trust me. It will only seem kinky the first time.

I wouldn't be surprised if you were Cambell's Soup, because you're M'm M'm good!

Do you believe in love at first sight or should I walk by again?

The Big Squeeze

It's 2 A.M. and a dimwitted drunk is sitting at a bar nursing his last bottle of Budweiser when he realizes he needs to visit the loo. Half slurring, he asks the bartender for directions to the restroom. The barkeep tells Mr. Sloshed that it's down the hallway to the left. A few minutes later, all of the bar's patrons are taken aback by the sound of a howling scream echoing down the hallway. Before anyone can make a move another scream is heard, and then another until finally the bartender runs down the hall to the restroom.

"What's all the ruckus in here?" he yells. "You're frightening my customers to death!"

From behind a door the stupid drunk yells back: "I'm sitting on the toilet. But every time I try to flush, something reaches up and grabs my privates!"

The bartender opens the door and stares down at the daft drunk. "I think you'd have better luck in the next stall," he says. "You're sitting on the mop bucket."

Politically Incorrect

That guy's belt just doesn't go through all the loops.

That boy's ten yards down and the game hasn't even started.

Warning: Objects in mirror are dumber than they appear.

What's Your Sign?

Neanderthal pickup lines.

Baby, you must be a broom because you just swept me off my feet.

I'm homeless. Will you take me home with you?

If I could rearrange the alphabet, I'd put "U" and "I" together.

Bumper Snickers!

CHASTITY IS CURABLE IF DETECTED EARLY.

I'M A JUST PRAWN IN THE GAME OF LIFE.

The Nuthouse

Some stories are so impossibly bizarre that it's hard to believe them. Of course if a nutball male, alcohol, and possible mental incapacity is involved, it's likely true. So picture if you will a fellow by the name of Leon Hollimon who was arrested in September 2005 for public intoxication while cruising around in a wheelchair in the middle of the road near a Lexington, North Carolina, hospital. No biggie. Police tossed him in the pokey for a few hours to sober him up and then released him. Early the next morning, an ambulance was stolen from a county emergency medical service, and what ensued was pure mayhem. The thief led authorities on a wild chase through three North Carolina counties up to southern Virginia. The vehicle eventually ended up in ditch when its tires were punctured. Who was driving the stolen ambulance? None other than thirty-seven-year-old Leon Hollimon, who was allegedly playing doctor, complete with stethoscope, pager, and latex gloves. Unfortunately, it didn't end there. When police opened up the back of the faux doctor's ride they found a very large, very dead six-point buck that Hollimon was apparently attempting to resuscitate. This was evident by the fact that the deer was given an IV and a defibrillator had allegedly been used. Hollimon was subsequently hauled off for a psych evaluation. No word on whether Bambi's father was actually resurrected.

Comparative Evolution

Single guy:
You look hot in that dress.

Married guy:
That outfit still looks great on you.

Stupid guy:
My mom has a muumuu just like that!

Quid Pro Quo

What you ask him:
Will you come with me to my family reunion?

His answer:
I'd be honored.

What he's really thinking:
Your grandma's a drunk and your uncle's a perve, but your cousins are hot.

Down the Hatch

Frat hazing rituals can prove to be deadly for pledges who fall for the stunt. Such was the case when a twenty-one-year-old wannabe at an unsanctioned fraternity house in Chico, California, died after being forced to drink over five gallons of water and then kept awake all night doing calisthenics while the other idiots poured iced water over him. Obviously, none of the fatheaded frat boys knew that excessive water intake and exercise can lead to a condition called *hyponatremia*, where the salt content of blood is diluted to the point that it interferes with brain, heart, and muscle functions which can trigger a stroke or heart attack. In the pledge's case, hypothermia was also a contributing factor to his needless death. In 2003, a pledge at Southern Methodist University in Texas passed out after enduring a similar experience. His boneheaded frat brothers propped him up, slapped him into semi-consciousness, and forced him to drink more. Fortunately he recovered—after being hospitalized for a week. There's no question that over-consuming anything can kill you, especially if it's being poured down your throat by a bunch of jugheads.

Monkey See, Monkey Do

Two men are sitting in a bar one night having a few drinks. The first guy orders a large blue margarita and quickly drinks the entire thin. He then wanders over to the window, jumps out, and slowly floats down two stories to the parking lot. A few minutes later, he comes back into the bar and returns to his seat. The second guy is absolutely astonished.

"Holy cow! You fell two stories, you should be dead!" he exclaimed. "How did you do that?"

"Well, this strange feeling comes over me whenever I drink a blue margarita," the jumper explains. "Every time I have one I just feel like floating."

Excited, the second guy orders a large blue margarita, and he quickly drinks it down.

"Way to go!" says the jumper. "Let 'er rip!'"

With that, the second guy heads for the window and jumps out. The next thing the bartender hears is a loud splat as the poor fellow hits the pavement and dies. The bartender glares at the first jumper.

"You know what?" he says disgustedly. "You can be a real jerk sometimes, Superman."

Bumper Snickers!

I SWEAR I WAS JUST LOOKING AT YOUR NAMETAG!

HARD WORK NEVER KILLED ANYONE, SO WHY TAKE THE CHANCE?

Criminal Minds

When Jeffrey Barber decided to play a practical joke on his wife, he had no idea that it would result in a fifteen-year prison sentence. Acting on his idiotic impulse, Barber fired a gun while at his home and subsequently poured tomato sauce on himself in an effort to make it look like he'd been shot. His horrified wife found him and called 911. As it turned out, the joke was on Barber because he was arrested not for his practical joke, but for illegally possessing a firearm. Apparently the jackass jokester forgot that he'd been forbidden to own a gun due to prior firearms offenses. *Duh!* Barber pleaded guilty and was convicted. No doubt his lawyer erred on the side of reason and gave up all thoughts of presenting a "tomato defense."

The Teste Drunkard of the Millennium Award

Take a moment to ascertain just how much you'd have to drink before you did something monumentally stupid. Something so bloody daft that it would make headlines and send you plummeting into the depths of utter and permanent humiliation. That said, most of us would think twice about sucking down that extra brew, a fact seemingly lost on a thirty-nine-year-old Exeter, New Hampshire, man who in 2005 was so drunk that when he passed out one of his buddies put a padlock around his testicles and snapped it shut. It's ha-ha funny, right? Guess again. When the idiot woke up the next morning his buddy was gone, and when he attempted to remove the blasted thing the key broke off in the lock. Did he go to the hospital or call a locksmith? Hell no! He tried to cut the lock off with a hacksaw. Fortunately for the knucklehead that plan was a bust. So did he have a Plan B? Nope. Apparently he wandered around for the next two weeks with that lock hanging around his nuggets until finally calling the police and going to Exeter Hospital where the padlock was removed by a locksmith. Luckily, he was released without any permanent injury to his little soldier.

Nitwits in the News

There isn't a commuter on the planet who hasn't at one time or another thought of sticking a dummy in their passenger seat so they could skirt traffic by moving into the carpool lane, which requires that more than one person is traveling in the vehicle. Some folks have used mannequins complete with wigs and make-up while others have opted for blow-up dolls. No doubt, thousands of folks have successfully gotten away with it. San Francisco Bay Area resident Kevin Morgan, however, didn't outsmart the long arm of the law. In 2005, Morgan was finally ensnared by the ingenuity of Officer Will Thompson, who apparently uses his patrol car as a step up for peering into people's cars as they drive past. And that was precisely how he caught Morgan, who had dressed a kickboxing dummy in a baseball cap and Miami Dolphins jacket and propped it in his passenger seat. The big problem was that the dummy's dummy was missing a pair of legs. Oops. Thompson spotted the disability and issued Morgan a $351 citation. Thompson reported that passersby were laughing at the daft driver during his interrogation. The other dummy was unavailable for comment.

WHAT'S THE DIFFERENCE
B E T W E E N
MR. STUPID
AND A COMPUTER?

YOU ONLY HAVE TO
PUNCH INFORMATION
INTO A COMPUTER ONCE

Criminal Minds

Can you see me now? After stealing a fifteen-year-old girl's new phone, her shoes, and all of her money, a pair of teenaged German hoodlums in Berlin apparently took pity on her and left their outdated phone behind. They forgot one thing though—the phone contained photos they'd taken of each other. *Duh!* After Berlin cops published the photos online, the story made the newspapers and was then picked up in television news reports. The father of one of the muggers had been answering phone calls all day because so many people recognized them. Oops. Disgusted, he hauled the naughty kids down to the police station where they sheepishly confessed to the crime. At this time it's unknown if the teen twits were grounded for ten or twenty years. One hopes that at the very least, they lost their phone privileges.

Stupid Says . . .

"Stupidity is also a gift of God, but one mustn't misuse it."

—Pope John Paul II